JUDGES, LEGISLATORS AND PROFESSORS

CHAPTERS IN EUROPEAN LEGAL HISTORY

GOODHART LECTURES
1984–1985

JUDGES, LEGISLATORS AND PROFESSORS

CHAPTERS IN EUROPEAN LEGAL HISTORY

R. C. VAN CAENEGEM

PROFESSOR OF MEDIEVAL AND LEGAL HISTORY
IN THE UNIVERSITY OF GHENT

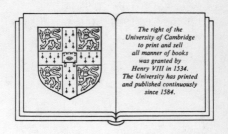

The right of the
University of Cambridge
to print and sell
all manner of books
was granted by
Henry VIII in 1534.
The University has printed
and published continuously
since 1584.

CAMBRIDGE UNIVERSITY PRESS

CAMBRIDGE
LONDON   NEW YORK   NEW ROCHELLE
MELBOURNE   SYDNEY

Published by the Press Syndicate of the University of Cambridge
The Pitt Building, Trumpington Street, Cambridge CB2 1RP
32 East 57th Street, New York, NY 10022, USA
10 Stamford Road, Oakleigh, Melbourne 3166, Australia

First published 1987

Printed in Great Britain at the University Press, Cambridge

British Library cataloguing in publication data

Caenegem, R. C. van
Judges, legislators and professors:
chapters in European legal history.
1. Comparative law.
I. Title.
342   K583

Library of Congress cataloguing in publication data

Caenegem, R. C. van.
Judges, legislators and professors.
(Goodhart lectures; 1984–1985)
"Based on a series of lectures given in the
academic year 1984–85 at Cambridge" – Pref.
Includes index.
1. Common law – Great Britain – History.
2. Civil law – Europe – History.
I. Title. II. Series.
KJC465.C34 1987   349.4   86-33353
ISBN 0 521 34077 2   344

CE

Magistro Sociisque
Domus Sancti Petri
In Academia Cantabrigiensi

CONTENTS

vii

Contents

PREFACE

This little book is based on a series of lectures given in the academic year 1984–85 at Cambridge, where I was living as Goodhart Professor. They were given to graduate students in law, as part of the LL.M. course in the Faculty of Law. Being based on lectures for students this book does not claim to be a work of profound research. On the other hand, the fact that the students were law graduates meant that I could raise issues in European legal history of a certain complexity not discussed in any exhaustive way in the learned literature. It also meant that I could assume an acquaintance with legal history and thus turn the course into a discussion instead of a monologue, and many issues prompted in this book were first mooted by students' questions. Since my listeners came from the continent of Europe, as well as Great Britain and the United States of America, I had sometimes to explain certain rather elementary facts of the history of the civil law to those who had grown up in the common law and vice versa. It is hoped that the reader will show understanding for this: a course on the history of European law, comprising England as well as the Continent, has, by its very nature, to take account of certain communication problems between the members of these two great families. I hope the reader will not be surprised to find that legal developments in the United States are touched upon from time to time: although England and America are separated by an ocean, the fact that they basically share the same legal system naturally leads the historian of England's law to be interested in its American 'transplant'.

I have been inspired to turn my lecture notes into a book by the interest of several colleagues in Cambridge, by the example of one of my predecessors in the Goodhart Professorship, John N. Hazard, who dedicated a copy of his own Goodhart lectures, *Managing Change in the USSR*, to the Goodhart Lodge 'as encouragement to those fellows who came after him to try their hand at a volume', and finally by the knowledge that it was A. L. Goodhart's desire that his Professorship would lead to the publication of a series of lectures.

The Goodhart Professorship in Legal Science was founded in the University of Cambridge in honour of Arthur Lehman Goodhart (died 1978), who devoted his life to the study of law. Although an American citizen, he made a brilliant academic career in England, where, after studying at Cambridge, he became one of the leading legal authors and teachers of this century. He was, among many other things, Professor of Jurisprudence in the University of Oxford and for many decades editor of the *Law Quarterly Review*. I hope it is not too bold to express the belief that he would have found the following comparative-historical pages, which freely move between America, the British Isles and continental Europe, interesting and to his liking.

I owe a particular debt of gratitude to Peter Stein, Regius Professor of Civil Law in the University of Cambridge, who kindly undertook to read the whole manuscript and made numerous useful suggestions and observations, and to the Master and Fellows of Peterhouse, whose hospitality I enjoyed as visiting fellow in 1984–1985. I also warmly thank Dr Daniel Lambrecht for his help in the compilation of the index.

Cambridge   R. C. VAN CAENEGEM

1

THE COMMON LAW IS DIFFERENT: TEN ILLUSTRATIONS

If amazement is the mother of science, the continental lawyer's amazement when he is confronted with the English common law must be one of the most powerful factors in the scientific study of the law (to which, after all, the Goodhart professorship is devoted). I shall therefore begin with the presentation of ten legal institutions which exemplify the different approach by English and continental law and, in the course of so doing, present some historical explanations or at least considerations. Many more examples could have been selected, but, whether under the influence of the decimal system or because of reminiscences of the decalogue, ten seemed a fair and not absolutely fortuitous number. As befits a legal historian, I shall be concerned with the historic or classic common law without, however, ignoring altogether various recent changes that seem to be narrowing the gap between the common law and the 'Roman-Germanic family'.

Some readers may themselves be amazed at this amazement: is it not natural that every country has its own laws? In the United States every state enjoys and even guards its own laws, and in some cases even a code of laws! To this the reply can be made that the difference between England and the rest of Europe (including to a large extent even Scotland) goes much deeper than the differences among the continental countries and the states in North America: it is the whole approach to the law and the very way of legal thinking which is different, and not just the laws on divorce or the maximum speed on the highways.

Nobody will be surprised to find that Chinese culture has produced a distinct legal system, because the Chinese world is a distinct civilisation, not only in law, but in religion, science and morals. The amazing thing about English law is that it is so distinct, although English history and civilisation share with the Continent all its main ingredients in the most diverse fields. England's language is of continental Germanic origin, enriched with continental French and Latin additions. Her religious history, in its catholic and protestant phases, is clearly in unison with the general development of European history, and the same is true of her political institutions: neither the monarchy nor constitutionalism or parliamentarism originated in England, nor were they exclusively English in later times. It is the legal system that is the odd-man-out and here no half measures prevailed: the differences are fundamental.

THE AMBIGUITY OF THE TERM 'LAW'

For the continental lawyer who crosses the Channel the surprises start straight away with the very word 'law'. He soon discovers the irksome fact that this one English word can signify two very different things. It can be used for a whole set of legal rules, whether based on legislation, judgments or jurisprudence (as in the phrase 'the law of the land' or 'the law says'), for which he uses the terms *das Recht, le droit, il diritto* or *el derecho*. It can also be used specifically for an act issued by the legislator (as in the phrase 'Parliament passed a law'), for which the continental lawyer would use *Gesetz, loi, legge* or *ley*. However, while he muses on this confusing terminology and smugly realises that his language disposes of two distinct words for these two distinct concepts, the continental lawyer in all fairness will have to admit that the *fons et origo* of his own law, the legal wisdom of the Romans, was not free from the same confusion: in the phrase *nemo censetur legem ignorare*, *lex* clearly stands for *le droit*, but the *leges* of the emperors clearly are *des lois*. He will also have to admit that continental people use the same word for objective and subjective rights (*le droit* as against *mon droit*), whereas the English use 'law' for the one and 'right' for the other.

But why does the English language use the same word 'law' for two such distinct notions as the sum total of legal norms and a particular enactment?

In the old days the English language used distinct words for 'the law' (in the sense of *le droit* or *das Recht*) and 'a law' (*une loi*, *ein Gesetz*). For the former the word *æ*, well known in several West-Germanic languages for the old, and originally unwritten customary laws of the Germanic peoples, was used;[1] the term was no longer understood in the eleventh century and was replaced in the manuscripts by *lage*. For this same meaning the term *riht* was also used, as in the contrast between *folcriht* and *Godes riht*, i.e. secular and ecclesiastical law. For law in the sense of legislation *dom* was widely used. The two terms, for example, were clearly contrasted in the Laws of King Ine of A.D. 688–95, which distinguish *folces æw* and *domas*, i.e. the traditional law of the people and legislative enactments. In later centuries we find for the latter the terms *gerædnes* and *asetnysse* (and also the verb *asettan*), the latter clearly akin to German *Satzung* and *Gesetz*: thus the Provisions of Oxford of 1258 were called *isetnesses*.

The confusion started with the introduction of the ambiguous Scandinavian term *lagu*, which meant both the total of legal rules (as in *Denalagu* or *Edwardi laga*) and a legislative enactment. It first appears in the Laws of Alfred

3

and Guthrum (A.D. 880–90) and of Athelstan (A.D. 925–*c*. 936). In course of time *lagu* replaced *æ, riht, dom, geræues* and *asetnysse*, and as 'law' stayed in general use with its present double meaning. Thus the Danes gained a minor verbal revenge for their territorial losses in the first half of the tenth century.[2] Linguists could explain how and why all this happened: the legal historian can only express his amazement that useful words are unaccountably dropped by the wayside in the course of the centuries.[3]

One consequence of this English ambiguity is that one is not even certain how to translate such a key expression as 'the rule of law'. Personally I would be inclined to render it as *le règne du droit*, but I have found it translated as *le règne de la Loi*.[4] This is rather amazing since, to my mind, the rule of law refers not only to enacted law but also to the legal rules of various origins on which the court protection of the individual is based. A recent French work on the role of the law in American and French democracy sometimes renders 'the rule of law' by *le règne de la loi* and sometimes by *la règle de droit*, underlining again the perplexity caused by the ambiguous term 'law'.[5]

APPEAL: A RECENT DEVELOPMENT

As soon as the continental lawyer delves somewhat deeper into English history, differences of a more substantial nature reveal themselves. Thus, while reading the history of procedure, he discovers that appeal in the continental (Roman and modern) sense was ignored by the historic common law. The term 'appeal' was familiar enough, but it meant something quite different, i.e. a private criminal accusation which normally led to judicial combat. What is understood by 'appeal' nowadays, i.e. bringing a case before a higher judge in the hope of obtaining a better sentence, was unknown in classical times and was, in fact, introduced in the nineteenth century. Although it belongs at present to the every day practice of English courts, there are occasional signs that the old aversion from appeal is not altogether defunct. This is, at least, the way I felt when I followed a debate in the House of Lords in 1985 where clause 22 of the Prosecution of Offences Bill (about which more later) was thrown out. This clause provided for a – very weakened – sort of appeal, by allowing the Attorney General to refer to the Court of Appeal for their opinion certain (lenient) sentences imposed by the Crown Court. The historic common law knew only two institutions that bore some semblance to the present-day appeal. One was the accusation of false judgment levelled against the bench or against the jury, the other was the scrutiny of the record of the case in order to discover a mistake (writ of error and writ of *certiorari*), neither the legal principle nor the facts of the case being at stake. The object of the writ of error is apparent from its name. The writ of *certiorari* was originally a technique for informing the higher court, in the course of proceedings in error, about the procedure in the lower court. However, it also came to be used in order to have the records of the case brought to the King's Bench before judgment was given, a procedure comparable to the continental *evocatio*.

The absence of a modern appeal procedure was a characteristic of all European law until about the thirteenth century. English and continental law then began to grow apart, as the former conserved the primeval tradition and the latter began to introduce modern procedure along the lines of Roman-Canonical science (a brain-child of twelfth-century Bologna). However, it would be simplistic to attribute the introduction of appeal solely or even primarily to the shining example and the irresistible intellectual fascination of Ricardus Anglicus's *Summa de ordine judiciario* (*c.* 1196), Bernard de Dorna's *Summa libellorum* (1213–17), or William Durantis's encyclopedic *Speculum judiciale* (1272, 2nd ed. *c.* 1287). The introduction of appeal is a political event, as it implies the subjection of lower, to the authority of higher courts, which is a question of power politics. The kings of France succeeded in establishing the Parlement of Paris as a court of appeal because the political unification of the kingdom resulted in the subjection of old regional rulers – and their courts – to royal authority: hence it was normal to appeal to the Parlement in Paris against the courts of first instance in provincial places. In England there were no such provincial courts of first instance: all the common-law judges belonged to the king's central courts, so that the hierarchical prerequisite for real appeals was absent. This, much more than the fact that the common law ignored the products of the Bolognese doctors, was responsible for this striking discrepancy between common and civil law. For the parties both the English and the French system had advantages. The fact that one's case was settled definitively in one instance by the senior judges of the realm can be considered a boon. It entailed, however, a truly remarkable centralisation of cases from all over the country which caused inconvenience to parties and witnesses. In France, which was that much larger than England, this might have been an insurmountable obstacle. Hence a system with local courts of first instance and the possibility of appeal, when desirable, to the senior judges of the kingdom was a fair solution.

ENGLISH LAW IS A 'SEAMLESS WEB'

Lawyers who like this sort of delving into the past will be struck by another great divide, i.e. the continuous nature of

English legal development or, in other words, the absence
of great catastrophes like that experienced by France at the
time of the Revolution. Certainly the lack of interruption in
English legal development can easily be overstressed in the
deeply conservative atmosphere of the English legal establishment, about which de Tocqueville had the following to
say:

> I do not, then, assert that all members of the legal profession are at *all*
> times the friends of order and the opponents of innovation, but merely
> that most of them are usually so. In a community in which lawyers are
> allowed to occupy without opposition the high station which naturally
> belongs to them, their general spirit will be eminently Conservative and
> anti-democratic.[6]

Famous legal historians such as Holdsworth were
inclined to see every new phase in history not as an
innovation, let alone a revolution, but as 'further adaptation' of old institutions. Nor is it surprising that they pay
scant attention to such revolutionary phases as the rule of
the Puritans and the latter's very innovating and sensible
plans for legal modernisation. Thus Holdsworth finds it a
waste of time to study their programme, because all their
novelties were thrown overboard at the restoration of the
monarchy, and Plucknett finds their advances 'premature'
and therefore not really worth studying.[7] It all depends on
the meaning of 'premature'. Some institutions and rules,
indeed, are so totally out of step with the times that they
meet a united front of rejection, but others are premature
only because of ingrained habits and well-entrenched
vested interests: what could be reasonably objected to the
Puritan desideratum for the introduction of English instead
of law-French in the English courts? And yet, it was thrown
out with so much else when the old world returned in 1660.

These reservations having been made, it cannot be denied
that to the continental observer, who is used to thinking in

terms of *ancien droit* and *droit nouveau* as two incompatible worlds, English legal development appears as a historic continuum. There is no obvious rupture, no wholesale wiping out of the legal wisdom of centuries, no division of the law into a pre- and a post-revolutionary era. In English law the present is never completely shut off from the past and its historic roots are easily perceived. One might even say that there is no sharp distinction between the law and legal history: the modern law of treason, for example, which is based on the Statute of Treasons of 1352, was applied in the twentieth century. In this English lawyers are very much like their Roman predecessors who, as one authority puts it, 'cite other jurists as authority with no apparent awareness that some authorities lived centuries earlier than others': 'the Roman sources treat law quite unhistorically', without any indication 'that the passage of time and new ideas have any effect on attitudes to legal rules'.[8] With few exceptions 'the Roman jurists were uninterested in and unmoved by history'.[9]

It has sometimes been thought that this aversion to a total break with the past is rooted in the English character. Against this, however, one can point out that no such reservation prevented the English nation from making a sharp break with its religious past at the time of the Reformation. The rupture between the medieval and the post-Reformation Church in England is as deep as that between the *ancien régime* and the post-revolutionary world in France.

The absence of a total break in English legal history over the past eight centuries does not mean that there have been no periods of change: English legal history is not a tale of utter stagnation. In fact there have been periods when change was particularly marked – in the reign of King Edward I, for example, when every year from 1275 to 1290 witnessed important new laws (although there was more definition than creation of law). The legislation of the Tudors was even more considerable and truly innovative,[10] and, while the Puritans had their way, the middle of the seventeenth century witnessed very interesting changes indeed, even though the Restoration wiped out most of their reforms and plans. The nineteenth century, especially in the decade after the Reform Act of 1832, set about the task of modernising the 'old Gothick castle' with great verve, although it is true that procedure and judicial organisation were affected more than substantive law and, as the example of commercial legislation shows, there was more codification than innovation in certain fields of private law.

Yet none of this legislation ever cut off the present from the past, nor was it intended to. Respect for old institutions sometimes overrode the considerations of pure logic. Thus at the time of the Judicature Act of 1873 the general feeling was that the judicial role of the House of Lords would have to go, since there was no logic in creating a High Court and a Court of Appeal and keeping yet another instance of appeal above the latter. Yet, to everyone's surprise and in circumstances that are not yet very clear, when the Judicature Act of 1875 appeared, the House of Lords was retained as the highest instance of appeal, above the Court of Appeal. Nor was its role that of a continental Court of Cassation, which 'breaks' the judgment of a court of appeal and sends the case to another to give judgment: the House of Lords gives its own judgment and it is final (except nowadays for appeals to the courts of the European communities). This construction of the two courts of appeal, one on top of the other, defies logic in continental (and many English) eyes, and can be explained only in terms of veneration for the judicial role of Parliament in the course of many centuries – in other words, as Justice Holmes maintained, 'the life of the law is not logic but experience'. Another example of this veneration for the past is to be found in the role – or should one say the rule – of precedent. That the common law is based on precedent is the first thing continental students hear in their course of comparative law, but few realise how old some of the precedents are. Their real age is sometimes revealed only by careful research, which may well show how a nineteenth-century judgment was in fact based on Blackstone, who had his case from Coke, who found it in Littleton and so finally in Bracton. This ageless character of English law also implies that disuse of an ancient right does not necessarily lead to its extinction, even though some people convince themselves of the contrary. A good illustration of this point can be found in the grave political conflict which arose at the beginning of the twentieth century, when the House of Lords suddenly threw out a budget from the Commons, although it had not done so for some 250 years and, in the eyes of many, had lost this right through disuse. All this shows that it was safer to abolish old laws *expressis verbis*, as was done in the Repeal Acts which, for example, left only four of Magna Carta's articles standing.[11]

The contrast with the Continent is striking. In the sixteenth century Germany 'received' the civil law, i.e. ancient Roman law and the commentaries of the medieval schools. This was a momentous decision, for it meant the replacement of the medieval customary laws by the 'learned laws' (Roman law and its twin brother, the learned law of the Church) – a move which was deemed to further the political unity of 'the Germanies' and to provide the country at a stroke with the best, or at any rate the most learned, legal system available. Even more radical was the effect of the French Revolution, which not only swept away the *ancien droit*, but the whole political structure as well: it destroyed the *ancien régime*. The very notion of an *'ancien régime'* is unknown in England and one can only speculate when 'the old world' collapsed there: was it at the Reformation? Or at the time of the Puritan Revolution and the execution of King Charles I? Or at the Glorious Revolution? Was it the Industrial Revolution that swept 'old England' away, or the First World War? No clear and indubitable answer can be given: what is certain is that in England as elsewhere an old world has disappeared, but it is not so easy to pinpoint the exact moment when this happened.

The *tabula rasa* created by the French Revolution, even in its very first years, was most radical: not only were feudalism, manorialism and tithes abolished, but the Parlements – including the prestigious Parlement of Paris – were sent on a permanent holiday. The old provinces – many going back to the territorial principalities of the post-Carolingian era – were abolished and so were the law faculties and the old law courts, including those of seignories and manors, and with them a thousand years of French rural history. Many revolutionaries wanted to do away with the law altogether: all conflicts between citizens were the result of misunderstandings, and there was nothing that conciliation could not put right. Nevertheless in the last decade of the eighteenth century several codes saw the light of day. They were philosophical rather than legal texts and had no lasting effect. They bridged the period between the law of the ancient regime and the great codes of Napoleon and are therefore said to constitute the *droit intermédiaire*. Napoleon's codes were much less radical than their precursors, and in fact incorporated a great deal of old Roman and customary law. Yet they were truly revolutionary, because their approach to the law was new, and the old law which survived did so only because and in so far as it found its niche in the *Code Civil* and the less famous codes of the Emperor of the French.

It is appropriate to reflect here for a moment on the consequences of this state of affairs for legal history as a scholarly pursuit. In France, the situation is charmingly simple. There is teaching and writing on 'Roman law', i.e. the law of Antiquity which collapsed with the coming of the Germanic nations (the latter used also to be called 'the barbarians', but self-conscious Europeans of the second half of the twentieth century have become less inclined to bandy about this term of abuse). Next to the professor of Roman law there is the professor of legal history: he deals with legal development from the Franks till the Revolution. All the other members of the law faculty simply deal with 'the law', i.e. the great Napoleonic codes and the piecemeal changes they underwent up to the present day. Thus three periods stand out clearly and logically – Roman law until the fall of the Empire, legal history until the fall of the *ancien régime* and 'the law', which concerns the present but includes the nineteenth century. The latter is hardly seen as legal history and therefore is sorely neglected: it is too old for the practising lawyer but not old enough for the historian.

In Germany the study of the legal past is dominated by the 'Reception' of the sixteenth century, which meant that Roman law became the law of the country (with the paradoxical result that till this day German law is more Roman and less Germanic than French law). A school of lawyers grew up, who naturally saw the study of the *Corpus Juris* and the great medieval commentators as their proper business. Their greatest and latest glory were the Pandectists of the nineteenth century, so called because the Pandects or Digest was by far the most important part of the old Roman texts. To them the study of Roman law was not a historical but a dogmatic pursuit, since it was part and parcel of the living law of their time and age. However, not all lawyers in Germany were happy with the wholesale abolition of the medieval, national heritage, and in the eighteenth and nineteenth centuries there was some vigorous agitation for the foundation of a truly German system, as an element of the long-desired unification of the fatherland. Hence German legal historians in the nineteenth century were divided into two camps – each having, for example, its own 'section' in the prestigious *Zeitschrift für Rechtsgeschichte* – the Romanists and the Germanists. They both studied the national past, but concentrated on its two different (and hardly comparable) components: the former, on Roman law as it developed in the Middle Ages, was received in Germany and further adapted there in the following centuries, the latter on Germanic law and medieval customs and borough charters, as the true witnesses of the German legal spirit. Germanists and Romanists were not only separated by academic interests, but were also involved in a struggle for the future of the law. One day, it was hoped, Germany would be unified and would have one common civil code: would it be German or Roman? When this code was finally introduced in the last year of the nineteenth century, it was a mixture of Roman and German elements (the former being predominant), and also contained many articles derived from the School of Natural Law (particularly the 'General Part'). This civil code took the place of all older laws so that both German and Roman law became the playground of legal historians, whereas the study of the new code was the hunting-ground of professors of law, judges and barristers. The difference between Germany and France is noteworthy: in France Romanists and legal historians were concerned with different periods, in Germany Romanists and Germanists were concerned with distinct but coeval systems of law.

The situation in England is different again. Since the common law is a 'seamless web', every lawyer may have to take into account some precedent or some enactment going back any number of centuries (in fact, back to the time of Richard I, the limit of legal memory). This means that every jurist who wants to study the merits of a case in depth may have to rove across the centuries and become a legal historian, or, should one say, a historical lawyer. Sir Edward Coke, who was possibly the most learned common lawyer of all time, based his writings and pronouncements on innumerable medieval texts, most of them manuscript rolls, which he had perused with indefatigable zeal. He did this, however, in order to find the law as it stood and had to be applied and, in so doing, sometimes was clearly hoping to find precedents that would suit his legal and political convictions. Thus he sometimes misinterpreted precedents to support his case, as was demonstrated with several of his 'precedents' in Dr Bonham's Case (1610).[12] This shows him to be a lawyer with vast historical erudition rather than an historian: for him the law came first and history was its handmaiden. Blackstone's famous *Commentaries on the Laws of England* are so full of history and their author is so aware of the past that they could easily have been called a 'History of the Laws of England'. Yet it is clear that Blackstone's aim was that of a lawyer, i.e. to expound, explain and extol English law as history had organically produced it. Legal historians are interested in the origin and development of institutions as they appear in the texts of bygone centuries: they do not in the first place want to ascertain a point in a legal debate. This does not mean to say that they are not 'engaged': they might wish to make a political point.

The reader should not forget that 'neutral' historians, who do not from the outset have a religious or political message, are a recent phenomenon, and even today are far from general. On the universal time-scale the historians who, like Ranke, want to narrate 'what really happened' with scientific objectivity and without taking sides, are a very recent species. For many centuries scholars served a dynasty, a Church or a party, some cynically, others with real conviction. This applies to the earliest legal historians in England. John Selden, who published the first such history in 1610, had a universal interest in the law, being a comparatist as well as an historian, but his parliamentarian and anti-clerical convictions coloured his historical research. Sir Matthew Hale, another learned jurist of the seventeenth century, had a clear message for those who read his *History of the Common Law*. It was one of national pride in the historic sovereignty of England, and if this implied denying that William the Conqueror had been a conqueror and the Conquest a conquest, then he did not hesitate to do so – in the most emphatic terms. He was particularly upset by the notion that William I's accession, often called the *Conquestus Anglie*, had really been a conquest 'as did, or could alter the laws of this kingdom, or impose laws upon the people *per modum conquestus* or *jure belli*'. So, as some ignorant and prejudiced people had entertained this notion, the author announced that he would 'rip them up and lay open this whole business from the bottom'.[13] In the first half of the nineteenth century we find legal historians, such as John Reeves (died 1829) and George Crabb (died 1851), who wrote in a purely antiquarian vein, neatly grouping their data in a simple chronological scheme and safely quoting their sources at every step: their works lack vision and are devoid of any literary merit. It was, of course, with Maitland that a new and modern era opened for English legal history. He was a lawyer by training, but a historian by vocation. He was fully aware of the progress of modern critical historiography on the Continent, had a broad vision and a lively and imaginative style. Having no axe to grind, he wanted only to describe the past with the greatest possible accuracy and comprehension.[14] He was certainly the founder of modern English legal history, but the activity of full-time legal historians in England does not change the fact that English law – and particularly the common law – is a continuum that spans the centuries. No modern textbook on English law is conceivable without extensive historical chapters and some are almost wholly historical in nature:[15] English law is the product of history much more than any system based on a codification which cuts sharply across the organic growth of centuries.

If England is unaware of an absolute divide between lawyers and legal historians, she is equally ignorant of a distinction between Romanists and Germanists or any other division *ratione materiae*. This is because the common law is so predominant that the other elements in English legal history such as Roman and ecclesiastical law are marginal phenomena. The study of Roman law gained real importance only in so far as it was relevant to the common law. Thus arose the controversy on the role of Roman law in Bracton's *Treatise* and the measure of his knowledge of the civil law, as did the question – largely provoked by Maitland – whether the common law was ever in danger in the days of the Renaissance, when some people thought that England would be well advised to throw her medieval and barbaric law overboard and adopt the *Corpus Juris*, which was turning into the common law of all civilised Europe.

THE RULE OF EXCLUSION

Lawyers who are less interested in history than in scrutinising the workings of the judicial mind, will find another contrast between English and continental attitudes in the – to continentals – most surprising rule of exclusion. There may not be another field where the 'rugged exclusiveness' of the common law 'disdaining fellowship with the more polished learning of the civilians' (as Sir Frederick Pollock put it in his inaugural lecture in Oxford in 1883) is more striking and strange. The rule of exclusion binds the judges to the letter of the statute and prevents them from delving into other texts – such as parliamentary debates and committee reports – in order to discover the intention of the lawgiver. On the Continent students are taught to go beyond the letter of the law if there is any doubt as to the latter's interpretation and to consult *travaux préparatoires* and similar texts in order to discover the true meaning of the law, i.e. the intention of the lawgiver. This is exactly what the English judiciary is not supposed to do: the construction of a statute is to be carried out following old judicial techniques of literal interpretation of its *ipsissima verba* and to stop at that. If this leads to a result that is the opposite of what the lawgiver intended, that is just too bad: the legislator should have drafted his text more carefully. The idea behind this attitude, which was a creation of the bench, is that it is the best safeguard against legal uncertainty. The lawgiver is a many-headed monster and it is difficult to find out the real intentions of the hundreds of parliamentarians who have voted for a statute, but the latter's text, so the reasoning goes, is incontrovertible and rock-like. The logical consequence of the doctrine of exclusion should be that the lawgiver is the last person to whom to turn in order to understand the true meaning of the law! This is in effect what Lord Halsbury said in 1902: 'In construing a statute I believe the worst person to construe it is the person who is responsible for its drafting.'[16] It is interesting to speculate whether the author of that pronouncement was aware of the exactly opposite statements contained in the 'common written laws' of the Continent. Both are as outspoken as Halsbury, for civil law says 'ejus est interpretari cujus est condere' and canon law says 'unde jus prodit, interpretatio quoque procedat'.[17] These two pronouncements incidentally reveal the venerable antiquity of the continental approach in this matter. But the English doctrine, although in its classical severity a product of the nineteenth century, can also claim great antiquity. It seems to go back to those medieval times when the judges were consulted by the lawgiver in the drafting of the statutes. 'Do not gloss the statute; we know it better than you, for it was our work', said Hengham CJ to counsel discussing the Second Statute of Westminster.[18]

When in later history the judges were no longer consulted in this drafting, they nevertheless continued to consider themselves to be the best interpreters of the statutes. They have done so, however, according to strict rules, largely developed by the courts, but embodied in statutes such as the Interpretation Act of 1978,[19] whose commentator, F. A. R. Bennion, has carefully expounded the criticisms of the notion that Parliament can have an 'intention' and has tried to refute them.[20] From the 1970s onwards the doctrine of exclusion, whose heyday was around 1900, has come under increasing attack. The last classic exposition was given by Lord Lloyd of Hampstead, who has no patience with the very concept of the 'legislative intent'. 'What is this?' he asks, and replies: 'the least reflection makes clear that the lawmaker does not exist . . . A legislator certainly has no intention whatever in connection with words which some two or three drafted, which a considerable number rejected and ... the majority may have different ideas and beliefs.'[21] 'When the legislature has uttered the words of a statute, another author writes, 'it is *functus officio*'[22]: preliminary materials have no relevance. That the result of this construction was sometimes inconsistent with the clear intent of Parliament did not shake the conviction of the judges.[23] At least, it failed to shake the conviction of some of them; others grew critical of the old doctrine, and the present trend clearly is to move away from it towards the continental approach. Nobody will be surprised to find Lord Denning amongst such critics,[24] and he is not a *vox clamans in deserto*, for Professor Friedmann talks of the 'sympathetic collaboration' of the courts with the legislature.[25] And Professor Stein writes that the judges have come to accept 'that they should pay more attention than they have done to the aims and purposes of a statute in relation to its social background ... They may, for example, look at the reports of commissions on which the statute was based in order to discover more about its purposes than emerges from the statutory text itself.'[26]

This was precisely the sort of involvement in 'politics' that the exclusion rule wanted to avoid.[27] There has been not only a spontaneous new insight at work within the judiciary, but the British accession to the Treaty of Rome also undoubtedly played its part: Section 3 of the European Community Act 1972 requires English courts to interpret Treaty provisions of Community instruments after the manner of the European courts, which means that they must look to the purpose and intent of the relevant texts.[28] In spite of all this 'modernism' it is interesting to find in quite recent statements that the old exclusion idea has survived in the minds of some important judges, even if it is perhaps not so blatantly formulated as used to be the case. I refer to a statement by Lord Reid in *Black-Clawson International* v. *Papierwerke Walhof-Aschaffenburg* (1975): 'We often say that we are looking for the intention of Parliament, but that is not quite accurate; we are seeking the meaning of the words which Parliament used: we are seeking not what Parliament meant but the true meaning of what they said.'[29]

A LAND WITHOUT A CONSTITUTION?

The jurist who is interested in public law and has grown up with his country's constitution at his elbow will be surprised to find that Great Britain manages to be a *Rechtsstaat* without having such a fundamental text. When we say that Britain has no constitution, we are not only saying that she has no written constitution, but that she really has no constitution at all, in the sense that there are no special, 'fundamental' laws that cannot be abolished or changed by Parliament like any other law, via the usual channels and with the ordinary majority required for any act of legislation. History, even recent, is witness that there is, for example, nothing or nobody to stop Parliament suspending *Habeas Corpus* or trial by jury in any part of the United Kingdom for any length of time, even though these two institutions are often described as a constitutional birthright. There is thus no escaping the pronouncement of an authority such as J. W. Gough: 'Law is fundamental when it cannot be altered or repealed by ordinary legislative procedure. In Britain today .. parliament is a sovereign legislature and there is therefore no such thing as fundamental law in this sense in the modern British constitution.'[30]

The continental European, used to written constitutions

that are not easily changed, and the American citizen, whose constitution is even more difficult to tamper with, are amazed to find that there is in Britain in this day and age no Bill of Rights, no catalogue of liberties outside the reach of the omnicompetent and even omnipotent Parliament at Westminster. This same Parliament can, of course, change or abolish all customs and all judicial precedents, for such is the meaning of its omnipotence. It is clear therefore that this absence of a sacred Bill of Rights is a direct consequence of the sovereignty of Parliament, especially the House of Commons. Through the bias of the European Treaties on Human Rights, certain rights are guaranteed in Britain as in the other signatory states and out of reach of Parliament, but purely within the British legal context the absence of a Bill of Rights is a fact. This has nothing to do with the common law, for the United States of America belongs predominantly to the world of the common law; nor has it anything to do with Commonwealth ties or ideas, since Canada has a Bill of Rights.[31] Nor has it anything to do with any lack of love of liberty in Britain, where the struggle for personal freedom as against overmighty kings is a true historical leitmotiv. It is in the history of English political institutions that the explanation of this patent anomaly in the present western world can be found.

The theory of parliamentary sovereignty, i.e. that Parliament is an absolutely sovereign legislature, is built on two pillars. The first is that no parliament can bind a future parliament or be bound by a previous one. There are no laws that Parliament cannot make or unmake and no consideration of morality or natural law can prevail against a clear statute emanating from Westminster. The second is that no judge can condemn a law and refuse to apply it on the ground that it is incompatible with the constitution or the fundamental principles of the common law: that would

21

be a usurpation of the legislative function by the judiciary. As is well known, this present doctrine received its classical expression in the nineteenth century in the work of A. V. Dicey,[32] Vinerian Professor of Law in the University of Oxford. Its historic origin, however, is to be found one century earlier. Sir Edward Coke, in the early seventeenth century, still held that statutes contrary to reason and the fundamental principles of the common law were null and void. He was frightened by absolute powers, whether vested in the crown or in Parliament, and wanted to place them both 'under the law'. He was, of course, well aware of monarchical absolutism, for in Tudor times the crown 'has discovered that Parliament could be used as a revolutionary engine of despotic authority under constitutional forms',[33] but we should not forget that Francis Bacon had called Parliament 'supreme and absolute'.[34]

Blackstone, however, in the eighteenth century, expressed the general belief when he said that no consideration could prevail against statutes: they had to be obeyed and applied, however unreasonable. This is the more remarkable since he expounded his opinion at the very moment when the American colonials professed their belief in Coke's theory and placed Parliament under and not above the fundamental laws and liberties of the citizen – with the consequence that the young republic received a written constitution and quite soon accepted judicial review of the constitutionality of the laws. The divergence between Britain and America can be understood only in the light of the political situation at the time. Coke had reason to be afraid of an absolute king and his parliament, and it was understandable that the Americans did not want to be utterly subjected to a parliament that taxed them without granting them representation. But the British property owners had no reason to be afraid of the Houses at

Westminster, which consisted of men of their own class: the Lords and the chosen representatives of the gentry and well-to-do burghers were not going to attack any basic interests of their own fellow property owners and electors. The Blackstonian creed remained unchallenged well into the twentieth century, when two important changes took place: the democratisation of the Commons (through the general franchise) and the degradation of the House of Lords, still mainly hereditary, to a secondary role in the process of decision making.

An omnipotent single chamber, elected by the masses, gives many people an unsafe feeling and it is therefore not surprising that voices are raised nowadays – particularly in conservative circles – in favour of a Bill of Rights, which would be an impregnable bulwark against the extravagances of the elected chamber. But, whereas forces on the left as well as on the right easily acclaim such a Bill,[35] a great divergence appears as soon as the question is asked who should be the guarantors of the respect of a Bill of Rights, for the left does not like the idea of the judiciary (seen as a conservative force) being the arbiter of the constitutionality of Parliament's actions. The debate on all these aspects is in full swing, particularly since Lord Hailsham, the then Conservative Party's principal spokesman on Home Office matters, wrote before the 1970 election a notable pamphlet, *New Charter*, which called for the convening of a Constitutional Conference and the passage of 'a new Bill of Rights' by which, except in time of emergency, Parliament would limit its rights to legislate to the detriment of individual or regional rights. And in 1976 he made a public appeal for a written constitution and limits on the almighty position of Parliament, which, he said, had become virtually an elective dictatorship.[36] His proposal has made little headway. Some lawyers argue that a Bill of Rights is a legal impossibility, since the only limit to Parliament's legal power is that it 'cannot detract from its own continuing sovereignty', in other words its 'continuing legal omnipotence'.[37] Others argue that it is superfluous, since the respect for the rule of law, imposed by the judges, is sufficient guarantee against the tyranny of Parliament and for the protection of the rights of the citizen.[38] Politicians, i.e. parliamentarians, naturally do not feel inclined to reduce their own power and hand over control of the law to the judiciary. For there can be no doubt that a written constitution, accompanied by judicial review of the constitutionality of the laws, would tip the balance of power heavily in favour of the bench so that, in P. S. Atiyah's words, 'the judges would become the ultimate arbiters of the powers of Parliament'.[39] If it were not for this power-game, the notion of a Bill of Rights would have made greater headway, since the theoretical case for its promulgation is very strong, being, again in Atiyah's words, quite simply the idea that there are 'certain basic human rights which ought not to be at the mercy of a government or legislature: people cannot be assumed to have granted away unlimited and despotic powers just because they have elected a parliament'.[40]

It is not only the threat of the dictatorial Commons which has alarmed some sections of public opinion, but also the fact that Parliament has become a real lawgiver, churning out year in year out an endless mass of new legislation. This used not to be so and notably in the eighteenth century, when Blackstone was not alarmed by parliamentary sovereignty, lawmaking was deemed a marginal activity of Parliament, consisting largely of whimsical private members' bills on criminal matters, and enclosure acts. It has recently been pointed out that in the eighteenth century law was not deemed to be something that was made, it just existed, and therefore statutes were mere 'marginal adjustments to the reigning state of affairs';[41] moreover many people still held that Parliament was under the law and that the law could not be manipulated.[42] These ideas were still widely held a century later. Lord Melbourne, Queen Victoria's early favourite minister, took the view that passing legislation was 'only a subsidiary and incidental duty of Parliament'.[43]

Whether a British Bill of Rights will ever see the light of day is a matter of speculation and not of history. The legal historian, however, cannot help being struck by certain similarities between the British predicament and that of the Catholic Church. For here too in recent times voices have been heard in favour of the promulgation of a constitution (including a chapter called *de Christifidelibus et juribus eorum*), but similarly progress towards the idea, launched in the wake of the Second Vatican Council, seems to have slowed down or even ground to a halt. The trouble is that nothing in the tradition of the Church pleads for or shows the way to a Bill of Rights.[44] In the English tradition also very little points in that direction but, from a medievalist standpoint, the reader should be reminded of the fact that in the Parliament of 1369 it was assented and accorded that 'the Great Charter and the Charter of the Forest be holden and kept in all points and if any Statute be made to the contrary that shall be holden for none'.[45] We know, alas, that various Repeal Acts left only four articles of Magna Carta on the Statute Book.[46]

Nobody will be surprised that in the hectic days of the seventeenth century various opinions on parliamentary sovereignty were voiced. Some authors were upset by the idea that Parliament is 'guilty of exercising an arbitrary power, if their proceedings be not regulated by written laws but by *salus populi*', but others believed that the idea of

Parliament's being limited by written laws was both 'destructive and absurd'.[47] Some, such as John Whitehall in 1679, were particularly upset by the idea that the common law might be dominated by Parliament, which meant bringing all men's properties into uncertainty and confusion, so that down went the common law and property with it 'and let the strongest take all'.[48] And so the debate goes on!

THE CONSEQUENCES OF PARLIAMENTARY ABSOLUTISM

A logical consequence of parliamentary absolutism is, as already briefly indicated, the absence of judicial review of constitutionality in Britain. In the widest sense 'judicial review' means any control by a higher judicial body, including, for example, the appeal procedure; in the narrower sense, in which the term is used here, judicial review means the control exercised by law courts over the constitutional character of legislation, implying the power of judges to annul laws (or to stop their application) as being contrary to some article of the constitution. Many western countries nowadays have judicial review – exercised by a supreme court with a general competence, or by a specific constitutional court – and it is considered to be a hallmark of democracy. Its absence in Britain, with her well-known democratic traditions, therefore deserves special attention. This is all the more so since the United States, whose legal system is largely based on the English heritage, has it and many European countries, whose political institutions bear the British imprint, also practise it. Before we enter into the historical circumstances which led to the American divergence from the British practice, it may be useful to point out that, although in a wider sense judicial review may be considered part and parcel of American constitutional practice, it is not to be found in so many words in the text of the American constitution. Judicial review was established by the practice of the courts, i.e. when the Supreme Court assumed that it had this power, in the case of *Marbury* v. *Madison* in 1803, in the days of Judge Marshall. This does not mean that the Supreme Court suddenly usurped a power that it did not have under the Constitution: many lawyers and politicians had been debating the problem and there was a strong feeling that the spirit of the Constitution placed the lawgiver under its provisions. The judgment of 1803 was given and accepted in that light.[49]

It is interesting here to point to another country that was faced with exactly the same problem, not so long after *Marbury* v. *Madison* – the kingdom of Belgium, which had given itself a modern, liberal constitution in 1831. This fundamental law contained not a word about judicial review, so that in Belgium too it was left to the courts, and particularly the Court of Cassation, to decide whether they should exercise judicial review or not. Not long after the promulgation, in 1849, Belgium's highest court of law decided that judicial review was not in its competence, and the final responsibility for the constitutionality of the laws was to be left to the lawgiver. It is interesting to reflect on this difference between two countries which both had a recent liberal constitution, based on the principle of the separation of powers. In both cases a precedent created by the highest court decided which way the country would go (and in both cases the practice created by those early cases has stood firm till the present day), and yet in one country judicial review was introduced and in the other it was rejected. Speculating on the reasons for this divergence is no idle pastime, since it may teach us something about the British influence in those days. Indeed I believe that his-

torical circumstances are responsible for the Belgian–
American divergence rather than the intrinsic merits of the
case: there were and are solid arguments for and against
judicial review. The argument for is, of course, the consideration that all organs of state, not excepting the lawgiver, should stand under the law and obey the constitution
and that the judiciary is best placed to decide whether or
not a particular enactment is contrary to the constitution (it
is after all a legal debate about a legal text). The arguments
against are the risk of judicial involvement in party political
strife and the idea that the chosen representatives of the
nation are best placed to take the ultimate responsibility for
the laws they pass (if they break the constitution, the
normal reaction of the electorate ought to be their dismissal
at the next elections).[50] In purely political terms, of course,
the option between the two courses is concerned with
power: it is the question of whether the lawgivers or the
judges have the decisive word in the state, and here, in the
last analysis, the reason for the Belgian–American difference is to be found! For, although the Belgian constitution
contains few literal borrowings from that of Britain,[51] it
was very much inspired by her spirit and, as has been seen,
already in the eighteenth century that spirit favoured a
sovereign parliament and rejected judicial review. In the
United States things are not the same: although some
articles of its constitution are borrowed literally from
English texts, its spirit is quite different, as was the mental
climate in which the young republic grew up. Different,
that is, from eighteenth-century Britain, although loyal to
seventeenth-century English ideas! Indeed, at the time of
the War of Independence, America had two English con-
ceptions from which to choose: Blackstone's theory of the
sovereignty of Parliament, or Coke's older theory, forgotten in Britain, but well remembered in the American

colonies, i.e. that acts that were against the fundamental principles of the common law were null and void. And since the American revolt was based on the notion that various aggravating tax laws voted in Westminster conflicted with the basic rights of British subjects, it is not surprising that America opted for the principle of parliamentary subjection to the great constitutional principles and for judicial review.

As has been seen, it was in the case of Dr Bonham that Coke expressed his views on this matter most clearly and forcefully. It is not surprising that the tradition-bound English judiciary, although it adhered generally speaking to the Blackstonian opinion, fought some significant rear-guard actions right through the nineteenth and even the twentieth century. Accepting on principle the ultimate supremacy of the lawgiver, the bench disposed of some peculiar ways of reducing his impact on the everyday application of his laws, for example, by reserving great powers of interpretation and assuming that Parliament never intended to go against the common law, unless it expressly said so. The meaning of these interpretative restrictions is not difficult to guess and, for those who were not good at guessing, Sir Frederick Pollock spelt it out in so many words when he said that the courts tended to interpret statutes on the theory that the legislator was an ignoramus who should keep his hands off the law as much as possible and that if he did interfere with it, it was the duty of the judiciary to limit the damage to the strict minimum.[52]

Coke's ideas about the unshakable principles of the common law were adapted to the American idea of the unshakable principles of the constitution, which slipped into the place of the fundamental principles of the common law. Thus James Otis, Advocate General in Massachusetts, refused to appear on behalf of the 'writs of assistance' (search warrants against houses of suspected smugglers). In 1761 he argued that such writs, even if authorised by Parliament, were null and void. This 'chief rebellious spirit' of the American Revolution declared, invoking Coke, that a tyrannical act, such as the Stamp Act of 1765, voted in Westminster without American representation, was void and unconstitutional, i.e. against the fundamental (customary) principles of the common law. Here can be seen the almost imperceptible *glissando* from the common law to a constitution.

It is interesting in this context to have a look at 'laws' which have been considered at various times so fundamental as to be out of the reach of the whim of the legislator of the day, thus protecting the citizen against the sundry laws issued by powerful monarchs or popular meetings. The feeling that not everything is in the hands of the ruler and that the citizen is protected in his fundamental rights and ideas about what is just, can be found in the most various countries and periods. The formulation of these inalienable rights and indestructible principles, however, has proved to be a most difficult task.

In Greek antiquity there is a reference to the otherwise undefined 'unwritten laws', invoked by Antigone against an inhuman enactment by King Creon. In the Middle Ages the *jus divinum* towered above all human enactments and was the universal guiding principle, high above the statutes that 'were made in the morning and unmade in the afternoon'. In the sixteenth and seventeenth centuries there are references to the dominant role of the fundamental principles of the common law or the *lois fondamentales du royaume*. In the eighteenth century the law of nature or the law of reason (*Vernunftrecht*) was deemed to be the pole-star for the lawgivers in all civilised countries, which would put an end to the ridiculous state of affairs that crossing some fortuitous frontier turned right into wrong.

All these 'superior laws' had two fatal flaws. Their content was never precisely defined, let alone written down in the exact language of a legal text. This is small wonder since different people have different ideas about what is 'natural'. Hugo Grotius thought that polyandry was against natural law, but polygamy was not: how many people would agree with that 'natural' distinction in our day and age? The other flaw was that there were no authoritative courts of justice appointed to apply these various superior laws: it was all right for medieval lawyers to point out that even the pope had to legislate according to divine law, but who had the authority to sit in judgment over papal laws? Only modern states, beginning with the American example, have solved this twofold problem by defining the fundamental and inalienable rights and principles in the precisely worded articles of written constitutions, and by placing the lawgiver under the supervision of the judges, whose task it is to safeguard the constitutionality of the laws passed. Nowadays many states have a written constitution as their immovable pole-star and give the judiciary the task of seeing that it is respected. This would seem to be the solution for an age-old problem, even though the courts do not always have a simple and straightforward answer to every question. Thus the *Bundesverfassungsgericht* had to decide whether legislation permitting abortion was in conflict with the constitutionally guaranteed sanctity of life!

THE HAPHAZARD DEVELOPMENT OF CRIMINAL LAW

Those readers interested in criminal law may find a look at the English and the continental approach rewarding.

Generally speaking in English criminal law there is less theory and no codification. On the Continent the theoretical *Allgemeine Teil* is conspicuous and contains, *inter alia*, the elaborate *Schuldlehre* or doctrine of culpability, which descends directly from the medieval canonists. Also, the Continent for centuries has known great criminal codifications covering substantive or adjective law or both, beginning with the *Constitutio Criminalis Carolina* of Emperor Charles V and continuing with King Louis XIV's *Ordonnance Criminelle* and Napoleon's codes of criminal law and criminal procedure. English development has been different, lacking the conceptual framework which professors are good at creating, and its history is mainly a series of haphazard changes, usually in the sense of adding new felonies to the existing catalogue and multiplying capital offences. A good example can be found in the eighteenth century when private members' bills introduced, on the spur of the moment and under the influence of local pressure (for example, after a series of burnings of haystacks), the death penalty for numerous minor offences. The criminal law of that time looked worse than it was, since crimes were so 'numerous' because general definitions were lacking – as in the *Lex Salica* where there are separate titles for the theft of pigs, cattle, sheep, goats, dogs, birds and bees.[53] The inhuman and terrifying consequences of this state of affairs were combated in a circumambient way, mainly by the use of legal fictions (the good old technique of getting round the law while appearing to uphold it). One way was for juries to put the value of stolen goods artificially low to save thieves' necks. Another was to extend the benefit of clergy to all and sundry. This old *privilegium fori* used to be a real privilege of the clergy; it was rooted in the Christian Roman Empire and had been the occasion of fierce struggles between state and Church.

Yet, by the beginning of the eighteenth century it had turned into a 'privilege' that everybody convicted of a common law felony could claim and thus escape the death penalty (being transported instead, following legislation of 1717). Hence there developed a second roundabout technique to counteract the first: to prevent the emasculation of the criminal law special laws were issued expressly making various offences non-clergyable – a movement that started in the sixteenth century but gained considerable momentum in the eighteenth. Hence to the unwary observer what looked like an increase in capital offences was in fact a restoration of an older state of affairs by excising the excessive growth of the benefit of clergy.[54] Thus English and continental history are utterly divergent: on the Continent there is a doctrinal development and a series of great ordinances and codes which span the centuries; in England, spontaneous and disorderly movements, often cancelling each other out, and a lack of doctrine.[55]

PROSECUTION AND VERDICT IN CRIMINAL TRIALS

Criminal law and criminal procedure are closely linked and it is therefore appropriate here to delve into some differences of very long standing between English and continental criminal procedure. I shall briefly touch upon criminal prosecution and deal at more length with the jury, that most distinctive palladium of the common-law world. I shall deal with the criminal and not the civil jury, because the latter never had a chance on the Continent, whereas the former went through a phase of great popularity there and, although now nearly extinct in its pure form, definitely belongs to the modern history of European as well as Anglo-American law.

But first a few words about criminal prosecution. Until

quite recently there was a real chasm between the English and the continental (and Scottish) way of doing things. I say 'until quite recently', because here, as on so many points, the English legal system seems to be on the move: a Prosecution of Offences Act which should bring English practice closer to Scottish and continental models received Royal Assent on 23 May 1985, with the aim of establishing a Crown Prosecution Service in England and Wales.

The historic approach to the prosecution of crime, however, was very different. The main distinction for centuries has been that on the Continent the prosecution of crime used to be the responsibility of an agent of the crown, called 'procurator fiscal' (as it is today in Scotland) or 'the king's procurator', who prosecuted suspects before the courts and tried to convince judges of the guilt of the accused by pronouncing a plea, called *réquisitoire*, in which he presented his arguments as if he were a barrister. He was no barrister, however, but a powerful official of the king, speaking with all the authority of the state. Vis-à-vis the accused person and the latter's advocate he was very much acting from a position of strength – an imbalance in the criminal process much deplored by English observers. The English tradition was quite different, for there the prosecution of suspect persons was the task of a jury of the venue, a jury of peers of the accused. They decided whether there was enough prima facie evidence to warrant a criminal procedure against the accused. There were thus two juries involved: one, the grand jury, decided whether to prosecute or not; the other, the petty jury, decided whether the prosecuted person was guilty or not. Both the royal procurator and the jury of indictment originated in the later Middle Ages, the former as a consequence of the growing role of the monarchy in the struggle against crime, the latter in circumstances which have been studied elsewhere.[56]

34

From the twelfth till the twentieth century the jury of indictment operated continuously in England, but in 1933 it was abolished. Its place was not taken by some continental-style crown-procurator, however, but instead a different and rather remarkable novelty was introduced, the Director of Public Prosecutions. He was indeed an official of the state, who had to decide, on the basis of material provided by the police, whether to prosecute or not – a role comparable to that of the *procureur* – but unlike the latter, he did not appear in court, did not plead there against the accused or request the latter's condemnation. This task was left to a barrister, an advocate who for a fee would undertake to plead for the crown against the accused just as on another day he might accept the defence of a suspect. Barristers were members of the bar and not state officials (although some might come to specialise in prosecution work). So much for the absence of a *Ministère Public* in England.[57]

It will be interesting to study the new Act and to analyse how closely English law has moved towards the Continent. In the history of the jury, it is the Continent that has moved towards the English model (except in early medieval times, which will not be studied here in any detail), even though recent developments again point towards a *rapprochement* between English and continental practice. Indeed, there is no doubt that the twentieth century has witnessed a notable decline in the jury, the greatest and most striking hallmark of English law for many centuries. The abolition of the grand jury (an example that was not followed in the United States) has already been mentioned. There is also the almost total disappearance of the civil jury from the practice of the courts in the last decades and, finally, legislation has repeatedly curtailed the role of the criminal jury by reducing the number of indictable offences. This was allegedly done for the sake of economy – and there is no doubt that the jury process can be very expensive.[58] It is worth observing that the criminal jury for which generations of Germans had fought so hard was dropped by the Weimar Republic for precisely this same reason: its exorbitant cost. Nevertheless the question as to why the cost of the jury procedure, borne in the course of many centuries, suddenly became so unbearable in our own time remains open.

In spite of all this, the present situation, even while taking the reduced role of the English criminal jury into consideration, still reveals a notable difference between Britain and the continent of Europe. Serious crime is still a matter for the jury in the former, whereas in the latter only Belgium and some Swiss cantons seem to have conserved the pure English model; other countries such as Germany and France have mixed juries of judges and laymen. A glance at the history books may reveal something about the reasons for this striking difference.

The main outline, which is well known, shows a surprising give and take between the Continent and England. The jury was a creation of the Frankish monarchy and, when the Normans founded the duchy that was named after them, they took over the jury as part and parcel of the native institutions (together with feudalism, the Church and the Norman-French language). After 1066 they introduced it into England, like so much else, and used it extensively in civil and fiscal litigation. Soon it was extended to criminal matters, first in the form of the jury of indictment and soon afterwards (mainly because of the crisis of the old ordeals) in the form of the trial jury, which decided the question of guilt or innocence. On the Continent in the thirteenth century, the jury gave way to the system of proofs contained in the Roman-canonical, 'learned' procedure, which was first practised in the Church courts and afterwards in those of kings and other princes. Even in Normandy, where it had been an important Anglo-Norman institution, the jury slowly gave way to the pressure of French royal policies, favourable to Roman-canonical forms of process. In modern times the Continent forgot all about the jury and enlightened opinion thought it an aberration to put the all-important question of guilt into the hands of an assembly of unlearned country-folk. This was the heyday of Roman law, its doctrines and procedures in absolutist Europe. In the eighteenth century, however, this very Roman law came under criticism, *inter alia*, because of its undemocratic, secret and authoritarian ways and attitudes. The system of the *preuves savantes* or *légales*, and in particular the use of torture (which had never been accepted in the common law), came under criticism and when the French Revolution broke out the old *preuves*, like so much else, had to go. The void was to be filled by an English institution, the jury. Some members of the National Assembly even wanted to introduce the civil jury, but the lawyers stopped this by arguing that in civil cases points of law and of fact were too closely linked. In criminal matters, however, the jury was triumphant, and the procedural institution which had originated in the kingdom of the Franks returned after so many centuries to the kingdom of the French (as it still was) on 16–29 September 1791. Napoleon conserved the trial juries, but placed their composition under strict governmental supervision, and there were special courts for a variety of serious crimes, and especially those of a political nature.

Throughout the nineteenth century the jury was a flag of the liberal movement. Thus, whereas it had been abolished under William I in the kingdom of the Netherlands (which between 1815 and 1830 united the present-day kingdoms of Belgium and the Netherlands), it was restored by the Belgian Revolution of 1830. In Germany agitation in favour of the jury was active and widespread and predictably triumphed with the 1848 Revolution. This brief outline must suffice here and underline my feeling that a history of the jury in Europe over the last two hundred years has not yet been written and would be a rewarding subject for legal and political historians.[59]

The present-day situation is hard to describe in general terms. It is clear, however, that the classic jury, exclusively composed of laymen, and sitting in criminal as well as civil cases, is in decline: on the Continent, except for the criminal jury in Belgium and parts of Switzerland, it has disappeared; in Britain the civil jury has practically fallen into disuse and the scope of the criminal jury, as we have seen, is constantly being eroded. Everywhere, the professional judge is on the ascendant, either sitting alone or sitting and voting with the lay members of the jury, as in France and Germany.[60]

One final remark should be made before leaving the shores of criminal procedure. There is indeed one field where continental and English lawyers tend to think that they are separated by a wide gulf – that is the absence of *habeas corpus* on the Continent. It is in England in particular that one encounters people who are misinformed about the significance of that ancient form of process. Put in a nutshell, the feeling of many Englishmen is that thanks to *habeas corpus* they are safeguarded against arrest and especially imprisonment without trial, whereas on the European continent the police can lock up anyone for an indefinite time. This is a caricature, for in matters concerning the police custody of suspects awaiting trial it is the similarity between Britain (and particularly England) and the Continent that is striking rather than the difference.

Indeed both in England and on the Continent subjects can be kept – and sometimes are kept – in custody pending trial for long periods, possibly extending to eighteen months (only Italy seems to be known for longer periods of detention), and both on the Continent and in England this police custody is exerted under the strict control of members of the judiciary. It is noteworthy that at the time of writing a proposal was being made to limit the remand period by statute in England, again after the Scottish model where a statutory limit of 110 days exists.

A LAW UNCODIFIED

We come now to the contrast that every lawyer in England and on the Continent recognises, the absence of codification in the lands of the common law. If common law stands for anything, it is absence of codes, and likewise civil law stands for codification. The absence of legal codification in England does not mean that codes were not advocated there: some of their most convinced apostles were English jurists. Nor does it mean that no attempts at codification were made: the criminal code of Sir James Fitzjames Stephen, for example, narrowly failed to become law. Yet in spite of innumerable pleas in favour of, and attempts at, official codification, nothing so far has come of it. In spite of the example of the rest of Europe, the common law is still uncodified: the jurists have not prevailed against the judges, who are the staunch defenders of the law as it is. It is my aim to delve a little deeper into this complex story.

Two warnings are necessary. Continental law has been codified only since the eighteenth century, first in countries where there was enlightened absolutism, then in revolutionary and Napoleonic France. Until then the Continent had lived with Roman law, customary law (sometimes written down and given force of law by various governments), canon law administered by ecclesiastical courts, and case law, which could be found in collections of judgments given by various important courts, ecclesiastical and lay, royal and urban. The other note of caution is that in the daily practice of judges and lawyers the contrast between common law and civil law is far from absolute: continental courts take precedents into account to a very large extent. This can go so far that the courts in fact disregard certain articles of the code that seem to be completely out of tune with modern habits and ideas, without waiting for the legislator formally to abrogate the articles in question. Thus I remember being taught in the late 1940s the *commorientes*-doctrine based on *Code Civil*, art. 720–22, as living law. Some time afterwards, however, the courts started to ignore it, considering that it was out of date and that it often led to absurd consequences; finally the Belgian Parliament formally abrogated the relevant articles by law on 19 September 1977.[61]

Moreover, certain articles of Napoleon's Civil Code, which is still in force in France and Belgium in spite of numerous partial alterations by subsequent acts of legislation, are so generally and succinctly formulated that their application in the variety of situations that life produces must necessarily lead to a great mass of case law. For although the principle remains that, as Justinian put it, 'legibus, non exemplis judicandum est',[62] lower courts are naturally inclined to follow the lead of higher courts (and there are even certain circumstances when they are obliged to do so). The best example of the considerable case law that can grow up around certain articles of the codes is provided by the law of tort. In England its general scope has never been authoritatively formulated and the law has been developed by a series of disconnected experiments by the

courts. In France and Germany the matter is dealt with by
the civil codes (*Code civil*, art. 1382–86, *Bürgerliches
Gesetzbuch*, art. 823–53), but the few lines devoted to it
there are so jejune that the modern law of tort is basically
pure judge-made law and its rules have often only a very
tenuous connection with the text of the code itself.[63] Thus
the Civil Code does not specify whether 'damage' covers
psychological as well as bodily damage or whether damage
to a person's wife is included as well as to himself – and if
the wife is included, does a mistress equally qualify? All
these questions, of course, have had to be solved by the
courts, so that in fact both on the Continent and in England
it boils down to case law. Nevertheless, it remains true that
the ultimate reference point on authority is different and
that (quoting Zweigert and Kötz) 'the common law tends to
the independence of casuistry (see, for example, the distinction between fraud and malicious falsehood), while the
continental law tends to the coherence of a system'.

It might not be superfluous to make an attempt at
classification here of the much-used (and abused) term
'code'. To begin with, the codes referred to here are
different from official collections of laws (and cases),
whether made with or without some rewriting or arrangement, with or without official authority. Thus the *Corpus
Juris Civilis*, the great collection of Roman law texts made
at Emperor Justinian's command in the sixth century and
published as law for that part of the Roman Empire over
which he held sway, was not a code, but a systematic
collection of extant texts, some old and some recent, some
legislative acts and some excerpts from the writings of
jurists. The fact that these texts and excerpts were arranged
according to subject matter and to a certain (or rather
uncertain) extent doctored and streamlined by Tribonian
and his team does not alter the truth that the *Corpus* is a

collection of texts and not a code. The same applies to the *Corpus Juris Canonici*, which is an even more disparate gathering of ecclesiastical law texts. It includes conciliary canons and papal decretals compiled by Gratian in Bologna around 1140, arranged in a systematic order and accompanied by very useful headings and commentaries formulated by Gratian himself, and various subsequent official collections of papal decretals. In 1917 the pope published the *Codex Juris Canonici*, which was the first real code of the Church. In various countries, large collections of statutes have been compiled which can be called codes only by an incorrect use of terminology: in Britain the *Statutes of the Realm* and in Russia the *Polnoe Sobranie Zakonov* of 1830 of Tsar Nicholas I (in 45 volumes, containing 30,920 laws) and his *Svod Zakonov* of 1832 (in 15 volumes), the former being in chronological order, 1649–1825, the latter a selection in a systematical order.

A real code is quite different from these bulky tomes full of old and recent laws in their original and often barely understandable versions. It is a new text, specially drafted for the occasion, containing a comprehensive and systematic exposition of the norms in some important field of law, promulgated as law and replacing all previous laws, customs and legal authorities. Within this group of real codes what could be termed 'conservative' and 'revolutionary' codes can be distinguished. The main ambition of the former is to bring a restatement of the law, understandable to the public, to clear up existing confusion, and to get rid of contradictions, doubts and uncertainties, all of which does not exclude a certain measure of substantive innovation: the great central-European codes of the Age of the Enlightenment belong to this category. The revolutionary codes, by contrast, are issued by people whose ambition is to wipe out the bad old laws altogether, to abolish some ancient regime or shameful phase in the evolution of mankind, and to make a new start, even to create a new world: in this category fall the revolutionary codes of the *droit intermédiaire* (see above) and the early Soviet codes. There are, of course, mixed forms (abstract models and ideal types never encompass reality entirely) and it seems that the great Napoleonic codes are of that sort: they retained numerous revolutionary elements (such as the legal equality of man, which the great Prussian code of the Enlightenment ignored), but reinstated a much greater proportion of Roman and customary law, some of it going back to the Middle Ages or even to the Roman Empire.

Almost every country in the world nowadays has its great codes of civil and criminal law and procedure. The exceptions are very few, but important – South Africa, the United States of America and Great Britain: South Africa, because its law is based on uncodified Roman-Dutch law and uncodified English common law, the United States because the law of the great majority of the states is based on the English common law, and Great Britain because Scots law is based on Roman law and on British legislation, which is not codified, and because England has steadfastly avoided codification. It is true to say that there have been partial codifications or quasi-codifications in the form of great comprehensive acts (on commercial matters, married women's property etc.), and various fields of English law were codified in India for use in the colonial courts. Nevertheless, the statement that the English common law is uncodified is true to the present day. And as there is no codified common law, so there has been no codification of statute law or of equity.

Before proceeding and delving somewhat deeper into this anomaly on the present world scene, a brief terminological elucidation may be useful. The term 'common law' is not self-explanatory and has a different meaning in different contexts. Its basic meaning of 'a law common to various people or provinces or countries' does not by itself mean much: it all depends to what people or countries the law is common.

The English common law was historically so called because it was common to the free people of England, who all fell under the direct jurisdiction of the central royal courts. This meaning marked the contrast between the common law and various local customs; in a later phase common law was contrasted with statute law, the one being judge-made and the other made by the legislature – this is the current, modern meaning.

There was, however, another 'common law' or *jus commune*, which referred to Roman and canon law, also named the 'common written laws'. This *jus commune* was so called because it was shared by learned lawyers and law faculties all over Europe (including England). It contrasted with the *jus proprium* or *municipale*, i.e. the 'own' laws and customs of innumerable countries, provinces and towns throughout Europe. And the civilians, who understood that their learned law would never completely replace local usage, worked out a theory whereby the *jus commune* offered the universal categories and methods of all legal writing and teaching, and was also destined to fill any gaps left in local statutes and customs. This *jus commune* was adopted or 'received' in Germany around 1500 and under the name *das gemeine Recht* became the common learned law of all German lands, i.e. the medieval learned law developed in the German law faculties and applied, not without undergoing local customary influences, in German courts.

To make things even more confusing, this elusive notion of *droit commun* is also known in France (and in other modern countries) with the quite different meaning of the law applicable to 'ordinary' crime as against 'political' crime, as in the phrase: 'there is extradition for *crimes de droit commun* but not for *crimes politiques*'.

The difference in England between common law (i.e. case law or judge-made law) and statute law (law given by Parliament) has just been mentioned. A few words may suffice here about 'equity'. Part and parcel of English law, Equity is concerned with particular fields such as trusts, and is administered by the Chancery Division of the High Court. It started in the late Middle Ages as a form of equitable jurisdiction exerted by the chancellor as 'the king's conscience' in order to prevent or set right consequences of the strict application of the common law that were deemed to be unfair or unduly harsh, or to give people remedies where none was provided by the writs of the common law.

This absence of codification in English law – whether common law, statute law, or Equity – will now be examined more fully. One does not have to browse through many history books to discover that it certainly cannot be explained by any lack of interest. On the contrary, it is surprising how often in England codification was mentioned, suggested and defended in the course of the centuries, and how able the defenders were and from what diverse social backgrounds they came. The discussion will have to be limited here to some highlights.

In the seventeenth century it was not Francis Bacon or the civilians but the Puritan revolutionaries who pleaded for real codification. Francis Bacon wished for a streamlining of the statutes and a coherent formulation of case law.[64] Civilians preferred the science of Roman law to the medieval jungle of the Year Books, but, as has been seen, not even the *Corpus Juris* was a real code. It was the Cromwellian revolutionaries who wanted the law to be codified in a pocket-size book, well within the grasp of the ordinary citizen. These same reformers, best known through the labours of the Hale Commission, wanted to replace law-French in the courts by plain English and to introduce civil marriage. It was all part of a great attempt to democratise the law and its organs and to curtail the monopoly of a few hundred lawyers, who had mastered the mysteries of medieval lawyers' French (unintelligible even to Frenchmen) and of the register of writs and the law reports.

It is not possible here to go into all the details of the reform programme of Cromwell's days, but some remarks should be made. It is surprising how little attention the great, classic, legal histories pay to this fascinating phase in English history – fascinating not only because there was a rare attempt to break the oligarchic nature of English institutions in favour of democracy, but also because, in the middle of the seventeenth century, it foreshadowed so many reforms carried out by the French Revolution a hundred and fifty years later. Even the pocket-size *code civil* was literally forecast by the Puritan democrats, for the early editions of the Napoleonic code were very small (and attractively produced) volumes, which citizens could easily put in their pockets: vast numbers were bought by enthusiastic individuals and it is amusing to think of them walking around with their copy of the code, to read in moments of leisure in the Paris parks, or reciting the articles on the power of the paterfamilias to the family by the fire in the evening!

Various reasons are given why this Cromwellian episode gets short shrift in the history books. It is said that it does not deserve lengthy treatment because its initiatives were swept away at the restoration of the monarchy. It is also said that the innovations were premature: but can one really maintain that the introduction of English as the language of the courts in the middle of the seventeenth century was premature? In France the Parlement of Paris had drafted its judgments in Latin until the first half of the sixteenth century, when King Francis I happened by chance to discover this amazing state of affairs and ordered French to be used henceforth. In England the vernacular won the day only in the first half of the eighteenth century.

This same eighteenth century saw the beginning of a massive and learned onslaught on the old common law and the passionate defence of codification by Jeremy Bentham (who coined the very word). It was soon after Blackstone had given the last great exposition of the historic common law that this attack was launched by one of his own pupils. Bentham defended codification in the name of cognoscibility (another word he coined), and felt that a law embalmed in thousands of cases spread over many centuries could not be cognoscible to the people. But how could one expect the citizen to live according to the law if he could not know it? Bentham's eloquent pleas, soon translated into French and influential on the Continent, failed to carry the establishment in England, where the judiciary strongly opposed them. Even so, Bentham had not preached in the desert, and one of his converts was the forementioned Sir James Fitzjames Stephen, whose chief achievement during his Indian career was the codification of criminal law. On his return he tried to do the same in England and drafted a criminal code (1878), which was greatly admired but nevertheless failed to get onto the statute book, because of bad luck with falling governments and lack of enthusiasm in influential circles. His critics alleged, *inter alia*, that a code would destroy the flexibility and hinder the growth of the common law by shackling the discretionary powers of the judges. The final discomfiture came in 1883, when the

Attorney General introduced the part of the bill relating to criminal procedure, which suffered strong opposition and foundered in committee.[65] After the Second World War various official initiatives for law reform were launched, including the search for codification, but until now nothing has been realised in that respect.[66]

The enumeration of all these foiled attempts at codification, in contrast to the sway of codification on the continent of Europe, naturally makes one wonder what the rock was on which they all floundered. Opposition by the judges was certainly a powerful element, but it would be strange if a few hundred members of the social elite could by their magic words have prevented a development advocated or deemed natural and even irresistible by the rest of society. Broader and stronger social forces must be at work here, conservative forces interested in keeping the law in the hands of the judiciary, not for love of the judges, but out of the conviction that the judiciary more than the legislator can be trusted to conserve the existing social order. The English bench is historically conservative because it was and is recruited from the ranks of the top barristers, who themselves traditionally come from the gentry and the higher bourgeoisie. This was brought about in a variety of ways: blatantly in the past, when access to the Inns of Court was closed by law to non-members of the nobility and gentry and more subtly in later times, when recruitment was made among the few who could afford a public school and Oxford or Cambridge education. It is clear that law made by those judges would be conservative and that property was safe in their hands. When legislators meddle with the law, particularly legislators elected by the masses, they are easily inclined to innovate, to abolish or to change laws – an ominous sign for the existing well-to-do and notables.

There are, however, several other reasons why codification has failed to make headway in England: through a variety of political circumstances the English mind has come to associate codes with all that is abhorrent.

Codes are associated with the Puritan interlude and the regime of a minority of military and religious fanatics. They are also associated with the 'enlightened despots' of the eighteenth century. Although 'enlightened absolutism' is a much fairer appellation than 'enlightened despotism' (which is anyhow something of a *contradictio in terminis*), absolutism is rejected by British public opinion and enlightenment is not a quality the said opinion usually associates with its governments.

Furthermore, codes were associated with the fury of the French revolutionaries, another ghastly phenomenon that hypnotised British politicians so strongly that for several decades no progressive measures had a chance, since they were immediately seen as leading to countless guillotines overworking in the public squares of London. These were the days of Lord Eldon (died 1838), who was Chief Justice of the Court of Common Pleas and afterwards Lord Chancellor. As an extreme conservative he was typical of the period and opposed all progress, except the abolition of trial by combat; he also held that bad precedents should be followed even if avowedly bad, because of the certainty of the law. It should be noted, however, that in this view he was far from being alone. Even Blackstone had said:

Law, without equity, though hard and disagreeable, is much more desirable for the public good than equity without law: which would make every judge a legislator and introduce most infinite confusion as there would then be almost as many different rules of action laid down in our courts as there are differences of capacity and sentiment in the human mind.[67]

Those familiar with the judgments and writings of Lord Denning, a strong believer in the occasional putting-aside of bad precedent, will know that this controversy is still raging in our day.[68]

Finally, codification came quite naturally to be associated with Napoleon Bonaparte, with whom Britain was involved for many years in a life-or-death struggle and who came to belong to that country's most cherished demonology.

Some readers may wonder why on the Continent, where conservative judges were not unknown, the codification movement has been so successful. It is indeed fitting that attention should be turned to this question – and the question also asked why, at least right to the end of the nineteenth century and even the First World War, such important continental countries as Germany and Russia, like England, lacked codification (albeit not because of the power and influence of the judiciary).

When one says that Germany had to wait for her civil code till the end of the nineteenth century, this is literally true. It does not mean, however, that codes were unknown in Germany. For the Prussian lands there was the old *Allgemeines Landrecht für die Preussischen Staaten* of 1789–92; various German territories had used the *Code Napoléon* under French occupation and the kingdom of Saxony had a code of its own. Furthermore, other legal fields, such as civil procedure and the organisation of the courts, had been codified in the German Empire long before the civil code was issued. For the late appearance of the *Bürgerliches Gesetzbuch* the political situation was mainly to blame: as long as Germany was divided into numerous states, a common civil code could hardly be expected – just as it would be unrealistic to try and introduce one civil code for all the continental members of the European Community. There had been, however, one serious possibility in the early nineteenth century: the various German lands could all have introduced the French civil code, which was already the law in several principalities. In so doing Germany would have had one common code, whose qualities would have elicited universal admiration. It would have been a second *Rezeption*, with similar advantages as the first: legal unity and the enjoyment of a system of great intrinsic merit. This possibility, although advocated by some, never materialised. Not only was German national sentiment averse to taking over the law of the enemy, but strong opposition was voiced against the very principle of codification. As the great defender of codification arose in England, which had none, so the great enemy of codification arose in the country which already had one (at least in a good deal of its territory). This enemy was F. C. von Savigny (died 1861), Prussian jurist and statesman, first *Privatdocent* in Marburg, then professor in Landshut and, in 1810, professor of Roman Law in the new (and politically aware) University of Berlin. In 1814, he wrote the *Vom Beruf unsrer Zeit für Gesetzgebung und Rechtswissenschaft*, launched a vigorous attack on the very idea of codification and entered into a famous argument with Germany's great champion of codification, A. E. Thibaut (died 1840). Savigny maintained that codes fixed the law at a given moment in history, whereas the law was by nature a living entity, moving and changing with the broad stream of a nation's ideas: the law was one of several expressions of the national spirit, the *Volksgeist*, and should be free to move with it. So far the modern reader can easily follow Savigny's demonstration and, in fact, Portalis, the most philosophical architect of the *Code Napoléon*, had expounded and countered this objection, saying that the codes ought not to be too detailed and should leave ample possibility for case law to develop. It is when Savigny addresses the question of where the 'law of the folk' is to be found and who is to determine what its content is, however, that the modern reader is in for a great surprise, for it turns out that the learned jurists, the professors of law, are best placed to ascertain this folk-law, a task that cannot be left to ordinary people because of the 'complexities of modern life'. Thus the professors, who in Germany were all steeped in Roman Law (Savigny himself was the author of the influential *System des heutigen Römischen Rechts*, 8 vols., 1840–49), were proclaimed as the natural oracles of what the people felt. In the background, of course, was the struggle for control of the law. In this case the struggle was between the professors and the legislators (the enlightened princes or the deputies of the people). Savigny was particularly frightened of democratic legislatures as in the French republic. He was a deeply conservative man, believing in noble leaders knowing the law best and speaking for the people: evidently professors of aristocratic descent, as Savigny himself, had the preordained vocation to guard the law. Savigny's ideas won the day because they voiced some deep seated anti-republican, anti-French and conservative tendencies of his time. As a consequence the learned law of the previous centuries remained predominant and Germany entered upon a phase where the professors of Roman law experienced their last and most glorious apotheosis, in the predominant school of the so called Pandectists. Russia also toyed with the idea of introducing the French civil code. M. M. Speransky (died 1839), Alexander I's principal minister, was its great champion, but suddenly the Tsar abandoned the idea for purely political reasons: he could not bear to introduce the work of his enemy as the law of his country. Thus Russia lacked a civil code right down to the fall of the Tsarist regime.

Strangely enough, in 1864 the French code of civil procedure was introduced, so that the country then had a code
of procedure but no civil code (although one is normally the
complement of the other): for its civil law Russia had to live
with the bulky tomes of collected legislation which we have
already mentioned. Its legal scholarship was strongly
influenced by Roman law, and particularly by the learning
of the German Pandectists. Needless to say, the attitudes of
the judiciary – in sharp contrast to England – had no
influence on this course of events.

Nowadays both the Soviet Union and Germany live
under codified laws, so that England is very much the
odd-man-out in Europe. She remained loyal to her traditional ways, because of the conservatism of the political
establishment and the obstinate opposition of the judiciary,
and in spite of the eloquent pleas of some of her most
famous jurists. This naturally leads on to the tenth and last
great difference between England and the Continent, i.e.
the insignificant role of the law professors in the development of the historic common law.

It is generally known that the English common law is a
creation of the royal judges and that the role of professors
of law and of theoretical study – 'legal science' – has in the
course of the centuries been marginal.[69] No contrast could
be greater than between this English development and its
continental counterpart, for there the impact of 'professors'
law' has been of the greatest importance. In fact, it is not
too much to say that there are large and important fields of
law which were created by continental jurists just as the
English common law was the judges' handiwork. The
teaching of law in the faculties of Roman and Canon law

and the publication of learned treatises and commentaries on the *Corpus Juris Civilis* and the *Corpus Juris Canonici* by scholarly jurists (most of them professors) have now been going on for almost nine centuries. Even today, when the codes have taken over the role of the two ancient *corpora*, the teaching in the law faculties and the doctrines expounded by their most eminent commentators are of considerable momentum and carry great weight, not only with students but also with the judiciary and the legislature. These jurists not only comment on the codes and expound them, taking into account the relevant cases, but they also criticise codes and judgments and work out theories and philosophies about the way the law is, or ought to be, developing. They are real *maîtres à penser* for the whole legal world: the mere fact that the names of the judges in important cases are not quoted prevents the cult of judicial oracles, so well known in Anglo-Saxon countries where the names of those judges who gave the majority sentence and those who dissented, together with their respective opinions, are publicly reported. Continental judges are anonymous and faceless, the great professors and barristers are not.

The traditional continental situation is the fruit of many centuries. It all started with the discovery in Italy in the late eleventh century of the complete text of Justinian's great legislation, which had never been promulgated in the West. Whereas in the past various parts had been known there, henceforth the whole vast compilation (a summing-up of a thousand years of Roman law and legal thought) was at the disposal of western society. Immediately the study of the Institutes (a short but lucid textbook), the Code (a collection of imperial laws and rescripts), the *Novellae* (or 'new constitutions', i.e. issued by Justinian himself to complement the Code) and the Digest (a systematic collection of extracts from the writings of the classic jurists) was started, with Bologna as its centre, the cradle of the great law universities of the Middle Ages. A version of the text was established there which became the standard form for countless generations of professors and students, the *Vulgata* or *littera Bononiensis*.[70] All this learned enthusiasm might have been limited to a small group of specialists and of academic interest only as is, for example, the study of Assyrian clay tablets and Egyptian papyrus rolls in our own day. In fact the opposite happened, for the study of the *Corpus* attracted the attention of thousands of students throughout the western world, who flocked to Bologna to be introduced to a legal system that was vastly superior to the local feudal customs with which they were familiar: Roman law appeared as reason itself, the ultimate revelation of a perfect system and the pole-star for all legal analysis. Three schools of Romanists succeeded each other, each with the *Corpus* of Justinian as its ultimate bible, but each with a distinct approach and order of priorities. The Glossators (twelfth and first half of the thirteenth century) saw – quite logically – their basic task as investigating the meaning of the *Corpus*. They therefore explained or 'glossed' each line and even each word of the sacred text using, *inter alia*, the technique of quoting parallel texts from elsewhere in the *Corpus* to illustrate the meaning of a given passage. They abstained from pronouncing their own judgments, their veneration for the text being too great, but they did proffer nuances by referring to parallel passages that seemed to restrict certain absolute pronouncements. They also abstained from referring to the law as it stood in their own time, limiting themselves to the ancient law as they found it in the *Corpus*. For example, a famous text, which has reverberated throughout many centuries in the polemics of the jurists, is a passage in the Digest that says that the prince, i.e. the emperor, 'is not bound by the laws' (in modern terms: the state or the government is above the law). Glossing this strong pronouncement, Accursius refers his readers to other passages in the *Corpus* (and one in canon law) which put things into perspective.[71] The meaning apparently is not that the emperor is supposed to behave in a lawless manner; on the contrary, it is his first duty to obey the laws which are the very basis of his position as head of the Roman state, but in the Roman political system no person or institution had the authority to sit in judgment on the emperor, for 'one can only be judged by a superior'. Hence the problem appears not to be of a substantial nature, but rather a question of political institutions and judicial organisation. Also Accursius, who was certainly aware of the power of popes to condemn and depose medieval Roman emperors, does not refer to this reality of his own time, because he operates only within the framework of the texts of Justinian. The great names of this school were Azo and Accursius.

The commentators of the fourteenth and fifteenth centuries built upon the foundations laid by their predecessors, but went one step further. They widened their horizons to take into account fully what the world of their own day was like and what it needed. They were realistic and understood that medieval customary law and legislation were there to stay and that Roman-based legal science ought to take notice of this fact. Hence they had their eyes firmly on real life and wrote commentaries and treatises that went beyond the strict limits of the ancient *Corpus*. Their work concerned relevant problems and went beyond the words of the *Corpus*, so as to be comprehensible and ready for immediate use in the law courts. They frequently advised parties and courts on specific problems or cases that were submitted to them (*consilia*), which completely immersed them in the realities and perplexities of their fellow citizens. But they always were and remained civilians, i.e. the 'counsel' they gave was based on Roman law and was full of references to the *Corpus* and its glossators. This school also came to terms with the problem of the true place of Roman law in a European society that had moved far away from the classical world: it developed the doctrine of the relationship between *jus commune* and *jus proprium* (as was explained above). The great names were those of Bartolus and Baldus.

The third school was that of the sixteenth-century Humanists. These jurists were part of the general intellectual movement and shared its enthusiasm for the return to the sources, aversion to medieval barbarism (in particular bad Latin) and love of the philological and historical method for discovering the true meaning of classical Antiquity and its writings. The legal Humanists wanted to re-construct Roman law and the role it played in Antiquity, which necessitated freeing it from medieval accretions and misunderstandings and developing a truly historical approach. This they proceeded to do and there is no doubt that they reached a deeper and more exact understanding of the law of Rome and the society in which it had operated. They also produced excellent critical editions of the *Corpus*, that were only surpassed by the nineteenth-century German standard text. Whereas this was a great service to scholarship, it was of little help to the practice of the law. The pure law of Antiquity was applicable only to Ancient Rome; the law courts of modern Europe could do little with it and preferred the Roman law as the commentators had processed it for the Europe in which they lived. Even so, many lawyers of the seventeenth century managed to combine the practical use of Bartolist Roman law with the deeper insight into classical Antiquity, which the Humanists had opened up. This was particularly striking in the Dutch 'elegant school' in the days of Grotius. The great names of the humanist school were Alciatus and Cujas.

All this learned activity could have remained the privileged pastime of a scholarly elite, who taught and wrote, in Latin, of course, in universities from St Andrews to Naples and from Coimbra to Cracow. In fact all this learning penetrated into the practice of the courts and affected the everyday life of the people on the Continent (and in England, but to a much lesser extent) in a variety of ways.

Canon law was the first to feel the impact of the new Roman learning, the neo-Roman law of the Middle Ages, and then to affect the life of the ordinary citizen. Soon it was recognised that no legal training existed outside the civil law faculty, so that every would-be canonist had to learn the rudiments of his science there. In the field of procedure in particular this contact went further than the methodological stage, for so intertwined were the forms of Roman and canonical court rules that in the twelfth century a new science arose in the shape of Roman-canonical procedure. From about 1200 onwards this was applied in the Church courts throughout western Christendom. Here not only clerics but also the numerous laymen who appeared before the bishop's official in matrimonial cases could see for themselves how a court inspired by Roman law worked.

Around that time certain areas of Europe where the old Roman law had survived in a simpler, 'vulgar' form showed themselves to be naturally receptive to the refined and revived law from the schools and began to adopt it. This was particularly the case in northern Italy, north-eastern Spain and southern France, all areas which were linked together by the Mediterranean Sea and strong cultural and commercial bonds.

Soon afterwards the superior courts of the kingdoms were reorganised along Roman-canonical lines and manned by learned jurists (or 'legists' as they were called, because they had studied the *leges* of the Roman emperors). The most famous example was the Parlement of Paris, founded around the middle of the thirteenth century, and a beacon for many other courts.

Not only were the courts with their judges and barristers thus being romanised from the top downwards, but the growing nation-States also began to introduce legislation based on Roman law. Thus Alfonso X, king of Castile and León from 1252 to 1284, promulgated his *Siete Partidas*, which can in fact best be described as a Roman law textbook in the vernacular.

In the later Middle Ages it became normal that all courts of more than purely local importance contained at least some judges and barristers who had studied Roman law abroad or at home (for the universities were multiplying and going from strength to strength). And if their wisdom proved insufficient, the court could always ask the *consilium* of some eminent jurist.

Soon there was a demand from the public ignorant of Latin to be introduced to this new product from the schools, which was so obviously touching more and more people's lives. One finds that from the thirteenth century onwards in order to meet this demand authors of customary law used the learned law as a framework and model, or even incorporated large chunks of elementary learned law in their works in the vernacular, and thus familiarised their readers with the new legal gospel. Numerous 'legal vocabularies', in which the layman could find a translation and an explanation of the learned terms that the new wave of lawyers loved to use so abundantly (and so devastatingly vis-à-vis simpler folk), came into being around the end of the Middle Ages.

In modern times this trend became all pervasive and the classic period of the Roman law domination arrived, when even authors of customary law had to make extensive use of civilian sources in order to be taken seriously, and when some of them were civilians in their own right as well as authors of customary law. Thus Charles Dumoulin (1500–1566) was not only the great commentator of the Custom of Paris, but also the author of treatises on such intricate Roman matters as the law of obligations. In England during this long period the role of doctrine, professors and legal science was very reduced indeed. The law was based on custom, which was revealed by precedent, so the judges, not the jurists holding forth from their cathedra, were the oracles of the law. Young people who wanted to take up a legal career did not go to a university to learn some holy law book by heart and hear from the professors' lips what its exact meaning was; they went (unless they sought preferment in the Church or a diplomatic career) to live in some Inn of Court and listened to barristers and judges, to learn their law by seeing it in action in the courts – in the same way that a youngster who wanted to become a shoemaker went to live with a master and learnt the trade by watching and listening and gradually trying his hand. The law could best be learnt in the courts, in the books that reported the pleas – the Year Books – and in the quick and lively altercations between judges and serjeants at law. It was not in books of Roman law, which were irrelevant, nor even in great expositions of customary law which made use of Roman learning, that the pupil found the sources of his wisdom. Bracton's *Treatise on the Laws and Customs of England* was a vast *summa* of the common law, explained by taking civilian learning as a thread of Ariadne, but Bracton's treatise was a monolith, and the generations that lived after it was written ignored it, nor did it find a continuation or start a school. This learned and clerical work was a blind alley and the great names of the following centuries, Littleton and Coke, found the material for their treatises and 'Institutes' in the common law, the register of writs and the precedents in the court rolls, in the Year Books and Law Reports, ignoring Gaius, Ulpian and Tribonian.

Outside the scope of the common law, Oxford and Cambridge, like all universities in the Latin West, provided teaching in canon and civil law. The former was necessary to staff the Church with qualified lawyers and it flourished until King Henry VIII abolished it as being too popish. He had nothing against Roman law and even promoted it, but the 'civilians', as the Roman lawyers were called, were never more than a marginal phenomenon on the English scene. They sat in a few courts that followed civil law, such as Admiralty, but their ratio to the common lawyers did not exceed one to ten, and they were not allowed to deal with that great preserve of the common law, that foundation of the fortunes of the leading families, the ownership of land. It was not until the middle of the eighteenth century that English law was deemed a subject worthy of being taught in a university – in France the national law had made its entry there in the seventeenth. New subjects did not gain access to the faculties easily. Charles Viner (died 1756) left an endowment for a chair of English law in the University of Oxford and it was with the first occupant of this Vinerian Chair that English law entered the curriculum. He was Sir William Blackstone, whose excellent lectures were the basis of his *Commentaries on the Laws of England*, justly famous as the last great exposition of traditional English law before the onslaught of the nineteenth century, with its Repeal and Judicature Acts. Blackstone, who wielded an elegant pen (something that can rarely be said of English lawyers – indeed it has been said that there were 'few law books an intelligent man could read without dismay or disgust'),[72] set out not only to formulate the rules of the common law, but to show their cohesion and to demonstrate that they were eminently reasonable and not just a heap of disconnected norms, produced by chance pronouncements in innumerable cases. After Blackstone the Vinerian Chair went into decline for a long time, because the occupants considered it a sinecure, a state of affairs common in the eighteenth century, when university chairs were sought after for their emoluments but were not deemed to involve teaching (at least by the beneficiary, who occasionally found a poor scholar who did the teaching for a fraction of the salary).

In the nineteenth century the idea of serious academic law teaching really gained ground. It caused an increasing debate, for the way it was to be done was far from clear or preordained.

Some favoured the foundation of law faculties in the universities as the most appropriate places for the teaching of English law. It is noteworthy that at a moment when the German law faculties were the centres of law teaching and enjoyed universal fame, in England this was only one of several possibilities and was far from receiving unanimous support. In fact, when Dicey became Vinerian Professor at Oxford in 1882, he chose as the title of his inaugural lecture: 'Can English Law be Taught at the Universities?' – a rhetorical question answered in the affirmative.[73]

Others believed that the Inns of Court were best placed to organise the teaching and study of English law. Although the Inns had admittedly lost their old importance and had become cosy clubs for lawyers, they had in the past been the schools of the legal Profession, where in certain periods English law had been taught and discussed – a fine tradition that could be revived. The truth was that until the Common Law Procedure Act of 1852 there simply was no serious study of the law at the universities and the old professional training in the Inns of Court had long disappeared.[74] Then things improved: in the Inns a scheme of education was adopted in 1852, while at Oxford a hesitant step had been taken in 1850 with the creation of a new combined School of Jurisprudence and Modern History, followed in 1871 by the establishment of a separate School of Jurisprudence.[75]

A third group advocated that legal education should be organised by the legal Profession itself, outside the universities, where young people could, of course, first receive some general education in broad cultural disciplines such as the classics, philosophy or history. The idea of the Profession, i.e. the organisation of the judges, barristers and solicitors, running its own law courses and setting its own entrance examinations to a legal career, is of particular interest now because in France, for example, something very much like it has come into existence recently, at least for barristers (France has an *Ecole de Magistrature*, which organises examinations, and the Bar organises its own admission-examinations). Previously, as is still the case in Belgium, the final diploma of a law faculty was sufficient to enter the bar or the bench, but now the bearer of a university diploma in law has to pass a separate exam to be admitted to either.

After much discussion the universities eventually won the day and law faculties were organised which, however, have only really become important since the Second World War: nowadays, in contrast with the situation of a generation ago, one can say that practically all young people who want to enter a career as a solicitor, barrister or judge go to a law faculty and obtain a diploma in law. In earlier days they would have had a university education in classics, history or even mathematics rather than law, which was considered too narrow and specialised for university teaching. This victory of the universities, however, was not absolute. A law diploma from a university still is no legal *requirement* for the Profession and, more importantly, the latter organises a year's study and an examination before students are admitted to it. The great majority now do that year after their three years in a law faculty. The old Inns of Court also continue to play a role in the preparation for a legal career, although that is now of less importance than the universities and the teaching organised by the Profession. The rise of the law faculties has, of course, lent greater importance to law teaching there. English professors, however, are far from having the prestige and influence of their continental colleagues. Their books tend to be mainly textbooks for students and even their more doctrinal and original works are not taken as seriously by barristers and judges as they would be on the Continent. The Law Lords in particular seem to take very little notice of them.[76] Nevertheless a change has been set in motion and it is quite possible that when the students who today go to lectures in the law faculties are themselves Law Lords (that is in about forty or fifty years' time), they may pay more attention to the professional books, and the learned jurist may at long last come into his own in England.

Can one think of a greater contrast than between the English universities of the nineteenth century and their German counterparts? On one side of the North Sea there were hardly any law faculties, and professors played a minor role in the life of the law; on the other, professors of law were so eminent and revered that there existed the remarkable procedure of *Aktenversendung*, i.e. the consultation of a law faculty by a law court, whose judges were hesitant about a point of law and therefore sent the documents of the case, asking for advice and binding themselves to pronounce judgment according to the 'counsel' given by the faculty. Who could imagine the High Court, the Court of Appeal or the Law Lords asking the teachers in a law faculty what judgment they ought to give? It is interesting, by the way, to point out that the famous Savigny in his Berlin days started the practice in his faculty of a *Spruch-Collegium*, an extraordinary sort of tribunal competent to deliver opinions on cases remitted to it by a law court. It was just the sort of role he found suitable for a professor: to instruct ignorant judges in what the law was and what their judgment should be.

How can this enormous difference between England and Germany be explained? Why this extreme contrast of judge-made law on one side of the North Sea and professor-made law on the other? This is the problem to which we shall now turn our attention, but widening it to encompass not only Germany but all the main countries of the Continent and to include the role of the legislator as well.

2

THE MASTERY OF THE LAW: JUDGES, LEGISLATORS AND PROFESSORS

SOME FACTS

The historical facts are not difficult to summarise. Various European countries have seen the control of the law pass through various hands, i.e. those of the judiciary, the legislature, or the schools. This is not to say, of course, that there were periods or countries where one such controlled the law exclusively: there has always been some case law, some legislation and some writing about legal matters. Only the fully feudalised era of say the tenth and eleventh centuries on the continent was almost totally devoid of legislation and legal learning. Certain periods and countries, however, have witnessed so marked a preponderance of one of these groups of people that it could be considered the essential 'maker of the law'. Thus it is clear that the common law was judge-made, that medieval and modern Roman law (which could be called the neo-Roman law of western Europe) was professor-made and that an enormous mass of French revolutionary law was legislator-made.

The reader will notice that there is here a connection with the traditional theory of the 'sources of the law'. These, as every undergraduate knows, are custom (as fixed and formulated by judgments), legislation and jurisprudence. However, 'custom' and 'case law', 'legislation' and 'jurisprudence' will not be treated as abstract intellectual entities, but investigated as the voices of certain groups of people expressing particular social and political forces in society. Thus, where most history books are content to describe the ascending role of legislation or the declining role of case law at certain periods in certain places, here the following questions will be asked: who were these legislators and who were these judges, what did they stand for and what was their contribution to the political power-game that is endemic in every society? Instead of seeing 'sources' vying with each other, people, pressure groups and classes will be seen struggling with each other for power: controlling the law is the way to control society. Some readers may find that this is flogging a dead horse, yet the traditional law books invariably discuss the respective importance of the 'sources' of the law, without asking who the people are who use, or manipulate such 'sources'. Here is an example of the way many lawyers see the struggle of influence in abstract terms taken from a well known work by W. Friedmann, who writes the following concerning the Savigny-Thibaut controversy (see above): 'Behind the practical issue of codification stood the larger issues of reason against tradition, history against renovation, creative and deliberate human action against the organic growth of institutions.'[1] And Roscoe Pound treated the common law as if it were a person who triumphed over a variety of enemies. These were the jurisdiction of the Church in the twelfth century, and the Renaissance, the Reformation and the threat of a German style 'Reception' in the sixteenth. The seventeenth century established the doctrine of the supremacy of the law, which was developed to its ultimate logical conclusion in America in the early nineteenth century.[2] Professor Hanbury, the eleventh holder of the Vinerian Chair at Oxford, also viewed English history as a combat between common law and civil law and stressed the important 'part played by Blackstone's *Commentaries* in the final victory of the English common law and equity over the civil law as arbiters of the destiny of the English legal system'.[3] So many triumphant battles fought by a system of law! Why this abstract anthropomorphism, instead of asking the identity of the people who fought these battles and used the common law to protect their interests? Who has ever seen a legal system fight and triumph over its enemies? When Professor Lawson, in an otherwise most remarkable book, talks of 'certain forces at work', he does not mention them by name and speaks in terms of mysterious 'types of mind' rather than of people and social groups: 'There are', he writes, 'certain forces at work in the civil law which are not usually present in the common law and which have produced a type of mind favourable to codification and these factors and type of mind are perhaps more important than codes.' He goes on to say that the history of precedent differs in the civil and the common law and rather obscurely concludes: 'this historical difference is related to the presence or absence of the forces making for the introduction of codes'.[4] Here the task will be to try and find out which concrete forces were agitating for legislation and codification at well defined moments of history and with what precise social aims in mind.

But first a summary of the main facts. In Italy, where the learned law and legal learning originated, the professors who held the key to the true understanding of the *Corpus Juris* were pre-eminent from the twelfth century to the end of the *ancien régime* and the advent of modern codes. In England, from the second half of the twelfth century down to the great reforms of the nineteenth, the judges made and controlled the common law, regarding legislation as an interference and a nuisance and bothering very little about jurisprudence. In Germany customary law as 'found' by local and regional benches ruled supreme in the Middle

Ages, to be replaced from the sixteenth century down to the Civil Code of 1900 by the dominance of the learned jurists, protectors and expositors of Justinian's holy book. In France the judiciary, the legislature and the authors have lived for most of the time in a peculiar state of equilibrium, neither ever completely dominating the others. Of course, custom as defined and fixed by the French courts was important, but a mass of customary law was also fixed and given force of law by the monarchy. This same monarchy was the supreme legislator and from Philip II Augustus onwards there was a steady stream of ordinances, which became really considerable from the sixteenth century onwards and sometimes resulted – in the days of Louis XIV and Louis XV – in partial codifications of lasting value. However, this royal legislation had to be registered by the Parlement of Paris before it became law and, although the king had the last word, his government had to take the 'remonstrances' of his eminent judges into account. Nor was the contribution of the jurists negligible. From the twelfth century onwards, when Roman law teaching started in Montpellier, there was no century without some leading jurist working on Roman law or customary law or both, and some of their writings – those of Charles Dumoulin, Jean Domat and Robert Joseph Pothier – had a direct impact on the *Code Civil* of 1804: jurisprudence was always something to be reckoned with in French legal history. In the Dutch republic we find yet another situation. Here, unlike in France, medieval customary law had not been fixed in writing and promulgated or 'homologated', nor was there any extensive legislation, certainly not at the general level of the whole republic of the United Netherlands, which was too federal for that. So the vacuum was filled by jurists, first and foremost amongst whom was Hugo Grotius, who created a new legal system out of an amalgam of old Dutch customary elements and the learned law of the civilians. This brain-child was appropriately called Roman-Dutch law. It was never proclaimed or given legal status, certainly not in the whole of the republic which lacked the central authority to do this, but not even in the province of Holland: it received its recognition merely because of its intrinsic qualities and its acceptance by practising lawyers and judges.

This extraordinary diversity, these striking changes from one country to the next, all within the western world, are surely a phenomenon that raises many questions, and none more intriguing than why it all happened. What was the factor that caused such amazing shifts in the position of judges, legislators and professors within this single orbit? It is to this question that attention will now be turned and certain hypotheses formulated and checked against the facts.

EXPLANATIONS: THE 'NATIONAL SPIRIT'?

A first answer, and possibly the one that comes to mind most easily, is to blame this legal divergence on the diversity of Europe's nationalities. The answer would then be that the situation differs from country to country because the character of the people, the national spirit or genius, is so varied: every nation has its own character and this produces a different national approach in legal matters as in so many others. To take a more concrete example, the Germans had a theoretical bent and the English were pragmatists, which led in one case to a law based on the *Corpus* and dominated by professors, and in the other to a law based on precedents and dominated by judges. There are, however, some strong objections to this view. Nobody will deny that Germany has produced some great theoretical philosophers, but it is equally true that the Germans have proved themselves to be great technical inventors and gifted organisers with a thoroughly pragmatic approach. Besides, might not the pragmatic and the theoretical approach be consequences instead of causes? Are law and government the fruits of the national character, or is it the other way round? The latter view was expressed by no less an author than J. J. Rousseau, who wrote: 'Il est certain que les peuples sont, à la longue, ce que le gouvernement les fait être', i.e. the nations in the long run are what their governments make them.[5] If a legal bible and the learning built upon it are the basis of one's legal system, one's legal approach is bound to be bookish and theoretical. The cornerstone of modern German law was the *Corpus Juris* and its medieval continuation, because of a political decision that had nothing to do with national character. There was no special affinity between the law of the civilians and the 'spirit' of the German nation; the Germans were looking for a unifying legal element at a moment when they made their last attempt at political unity for four centuries. Up until the end of the Middle Ages, the Germans had shown no special aptitude for, or interest in, Roman law. The latter was quite patently the preserve of the Italians, who ran Roman and canon law as they ran the Church. It has been estimated that the medio-Roman law was produced by some 90% Italians and 6% Frenchmen, while Spaniards, Germans and Englishmen took about 1% each. It is striking how these 'national characteristics' appear to change with the times. The Italians lost their leading role in jurisprudence in modern times and Germany, whose medieval contribution had been inconspicuous, became prominent then, and in the nineteenth century even took the lead, so that all Europe had to learn German to read the great legal historians and Pandectists.

EXPLANATIONS: AUTHORITARIAN ROMAN LAW AND DEMOCRATIC ENGLAND?

A second hypothesis could be adopted to try to approach the problem from a different angle, that of some innate political bias of Roman law and certain ingrained national traditions. To put the hypothesis in less Sibylline terms: the idea would be that England and her law and constitution are democratic, while the continental tradition is undemocratic, authoritarian and absolutist, hence the success of Roman law (which, certainly since the days of the Dominate, was autocratic) on the Continent and its failure in England. Or putting it more briefly: 'democratic England rejected the authoritarianism of Roman law'. Many great historians, as is well known, have held the view that the civil law is incompatible with freedom. One quotation, from nobody less than Bishop Stubbs, the great Oxford medievalist of the nineteenth century, will suffice here. He wrote in a letter to the historian J. R. Green: 'The civil law ... has been one of the greatest obstacles to national development in Europe and a most pliant tool of oppression. I suppose that no nation using the civil law has ever made its way to freedom: whilst whenever it has been introduced the extinction of popular liberties has followed sooner or later.'[6] Let us check one by one the two points in our hypothesis. Is Roman law authoritarian? Is the English legal tradition democratic?

The first question is easily answered. Roman law at the time of Justinian had been imbued with oriental despotism for several centuries. The Empire was over-centralised and over-autocratic. The principles expressed in the famous phrases 'princeps legibus solutus' and 'quod principi placuit legis habet vigorem'[7] are eloquent enough, and so is

73

the theory of the *lex regia*, i.e. that in the past the Roman people had transferred their sovereignty irrevocably to their rulers. In the law of the imperial state, there is no trace of direct or indirect democracy. Certainly not in the late imperial Senate which was packed with the emperor's cronies and given to endless acclamations and exclamations such as 'Hail Caesar, through you we hold our honours, through you our property, through you everything'.[8]

The second question, as to whether the common law tradition is democratic, is more difficult to answer and I propose to have a separate look at various elements. Originally, and long afterwards, the common law was concerned with the feudal class of free tenants, for it dealt with the central question of feudalism: who ought to hold what from whom and for what service? Feudal law was not familiar with the Roman idea of absolute property rights, but was produced by the two-pronged idea that one held something (the real element) from somebody with whom one had established a special relationship (the personal element). This original English – or rather Anglo-Norman – common law was the law of a knightly class, and the royal court's main preoccupation was to keep peace between the king's military forces and to settle their disputes in a judicial way rather than have them at each other's throats over quarrels for land. Smallholders and burgesses had little to do with it and the unfree – in the twelfth and thirteenth centuries still a sizeable proportion of the population – were completely ignored, except for the writ of naifty, taken out by a lord who wanted the return of his runaway serf. It is clear, therefore, that the common law was not democratic in origin, but it was not autocratic either, since it was based on feudal custom, to which the vassalitic nexus was central. This relation was not based on one-sided subjection but on a free contract which created mutual rights and duties. Even the king, the head of the feudal pyramid, had duties towards his men, had to respect their rights and was always obliged to take their counsel. If he did not, the tenants' *jus resistendi* came into play, and that this was not mere theory was well demonstrated in the days of King John. So this law of the military elite, the custom of the landowners, was neither authoritarian nor democratic, but oligarchic.

What was the political structure of historic England? As far as the king was a feudal overlord it was bound to be oligarchic, but as far as the king was a ruler, placed over his subjects by God's grace, it was monarchic and autocratic. This dual nature of medieval kingship, the *monarchie féodale*, to quote the title of C. Petit-Dutaillis' famous work, belonged to its very essence, and it is not surprising therefore that in the course of history one finds the two elements, the autocratic and the feudal, vying with each other. From the Conqueror to King John, the monarchic, authoritarian element prevailed (except for the interlude under King Stephen), but John overplayed his hand and the insurrection at the end of his reign ushered in a period of baronial revolts, while the rise of Parliament in the four-teenth and fifteenth centuries led to a condominium that owed more to the feudal than to the autocratic tradition – it was, of course, also influenced by new European ideas about representative forms of government. The late medi-eval parliament could in no way be described as demo-cratic, since it represented only electors – in so far as it was elected – who belonged to the landed gentry and the urban leadership. In the sixteenth century autocracy had the upper hand again, but the oligarchy won the day in the seventeenth, and ruled supreme until the rise of democracy in the twentieth. The old theorists liked to represent the English constitution as a happy combination of monarchy, aristocracy and democracy, in which the aristocratic element was the House of Lords and the democratic the House of Commons,[9] but it takes a lot of goodwill to see the representatives of the gentry and the ruling burgesses as a democratic element – a measure of goodwill which they could expect from their contemporaries, but is too much to ask from the more critical readers in our own day and age.

What about legislation in historic England? Was that democratic? The answer must be negative. The general public had no part in the legislative process. There was no referendum and even the more 'democratic' chamber of Parliament could by no stretch of imagination be considered to represent 'the people': not only did nobody below the 40 shilling freehold have the vote, but also the Lords, right through the nineteenth century, were always ready to scotch any democratic extravagances of the other House. Legislation was the task not of the people, but of the king in Parliament. And in the development of the common law it was less important than the patient work of the judges who were weaving its timeless and seamless web.

Was this 'judgment-finding' in the common-law courts and the other central organs of justice democratic? Again the answer on the whole must be negative, although some doors were ajar for ordinary people. Certainly in the English judicial tradition there was nothing like the mass assemblies of the Athenian democracy. Popular justice like the people's courts on the agora was unknown. Nor were the judges ever elected by the people. They were appointed from the ranks of successful serjeants at law, an intellectual elite who had gone through many years of training and success at the bar and whose recruitment was at certain times limited by law to the sons of the aristocracy and the gentry. There was, however, a popular element in the jury (even though it was limited to landholders), for the judges had to put the important question of fact to them, at least in the common law courts, and this had to be done in terms that were understandable to the layman and free from the esoteric jargon that judges and serjeants used among themselves. Another democratic element was the openness of the proceedings, although it should not be forgotten that the dealings of the court were held in a very strange language – a medieval provincial French dialect – and were therefore quite inaccessible to all except a few dozen initiated. Also the very high cost of litigation to this day has been a severe hurdle for those who decide to take their case to law. Nor was justice easily accessible in geographical terms because of the excessive centralisation of the courts and their activities in London – one of the complaints the Puritan reformers wanted to tackle. Another criterion of the democratic nature of a legal system is, of course, its cognoscibility. On this point, the common law scored very badly, for it was and is uncodified, buried in a 'myriad of precedent, that wilderness of single instances',[10] and even worse, in the bosom of the judges who guarded the unwritten fundamental principles of the common law, against which not even clearly formulated statutes stood a chance – a situation remindful of the Roman patriciate who kept the *formulae* of the law secret. Might the justices of the peace have provided a democratic element? Hardly, since these traditional rulers of the countryside, administrators as well as judges, who dominated rural England until the elected County councils were introduced in the second half of the nineteenth century, were unpaid servants of the state, who, by this very fact, had to be recruited from the well-to-do leisured class (as the magistrates still are to some extent today), so that their oligarchic character is pronounced and evident. The conclusion must be that the profile of the historic common law and its administration is clearly aristocratic or oligarchic, but not democratic.[11]

There was under Cromwell a short but highly significant period when a conscious attempt was made to democratise English law and a commission was set up to that end under the guidance of a famous common lawyer, Sir Matthew Hale (died 1676).[12] The Hale Commission, sitting in revolutionary times and keen on getting down to sweeping reform (at least some members were), launched into outspoken criticism of the existing state of affairs and made drastic plans for change, which included the following. The Commission found that the law was a hodge-podge, too vast to be known, self-contradictory, irrational and absurd, of difficult access and couched in barbaric language – hence the demand for formulation in 'plain English'. The Commission obviously liked plain speech as much as plain English and the lawyers who served and perpetuated this defective law shared its condemnation: they were 'vermin' and a plague on their land, 'this poor nation'.

There were not only recriminations, but also precise demands for reforms, which have a very modern ring. The abolition of tithes was requested (John Selden had shown that they were not imposed by divine right) and also the decentralisation of justice. Strong local courts were to be established and such county judicatures were to be staffed by elected laymen. Legal aid was to be organised for the poor, the illegible court hand was to disappear, as was imprisonment for debt, and civil as opposed to ecclesiastical marriage was to be introduced. It is interesting to reflect that today, more than three hundred years later, tithes have not yet been abolished (although the Office of Tithes will in fact take them all out of circulation one day), decentralisation has recently taken some timid steps forward, imprisonment for debt was abolished in the nineteenth century (except in certain specific circumstances) and quite recently civil marriages in England have become more numerous than church weddings. The momentous demand that the law should be codified, with no scope being left for judicial interpretation, and that (as has been mentioned before) the 'great volumes of law would come reduced into the volume of a pocket book' so that there would be 'one plain, complete and methodical treatise or abridgment of the whole common and statute law to which all cases might be referred', was the voice of one clamouring in the desert.

Although in the long run some of these desiderata were realised to some extent, in the seventeenth century nothing came of them. Some people would say that this was because of shortage of time. But that certainly cannot be the reason, if one realises what sweeping reforms the French Revolution brought about in the same time-span of about ten years: when the political will is there, old institutions crumble as in a whirlwind and new improvisations arise every day. Other factors worked against the Puritans for it was not even as if the Restoration had to sweep away so many changes, since little had been realised in the years when the reformers were in power. Some of these other factors are not difficult to pinpoint: the leading lawyers (even in the reforming commission) did not want legal business, that from time immemorial had been conducted in London, to be transferred to the provinces, which would make their lives very uncomfortable indeed, while the well-to-do burghers, who were possibly the core of the Puritan movement, were afraid that a legal revolution might easily be the harbinger of a social revolution. They had not fought absolutism and defended their property against random taxation to see it fall into the hands of Levellers and Diggers.[13] The conclusion must be that the common law was oligarchic rather than democratic, so that our second hypothesis must also be given up, for even if Roman law was autocratic, English law was not democratic, except during short and untypical episodes.

Before formulating a third hypothesis, I would like to come back to the autocratic character of Roman law, because I feel this contention is not so straightforward and obvious as it looks at first sight. That the Empire was an absolutist monarchy is clear enough, but the disturbing thing for the historian is that the success of Roman law did not automatically and necessarily lead to autocracy (and here I take issue with Stubbs). Is it not striking that the country where Roman law exerted the greatest influence in the centuries after its 'rebirth', northern Italy, was the country *par excellence* of the free cities and of the most advanced experiments in democratic government, especially in Florence, and that nowhere else was the autocratic power of the neo-Roman empire of the Ottonians, the Salians and the Hohenstaufen so utterly rejected?

To understand this one must penetrate somewhat deeper into the medieval way of using and citing venerable texts – and also, of course, realise that political institutions are the result of struggles for power and not of quotations from learned authors. The *Corpus Juris*, because of the medieval habit of citing phrases out of context, could be used in favour of representative forms of government as well as autocratic rule: in other words the *Corpus* could be bent in several directions. For example, it is true that Justinian said that the emperor's pleasure was law, but he also said, in a famous phrase, 'quod omnes tangit ab omnibus approbetur'. What better slogan could one wish to defend democracy, direct or indirect, than the line 'what concerns all, should be approved by all'? So public affairs, i.e. everything concerning the whole community, must be put to the test of the approval of the whole community, or at least its chosen representatives! The snag with this much used quotation was that in the *Corpus Juris* it was not concerned with affairs of state at all, but with an institution of private law, the organisation of tutelage and more particularly the need to obtain the approval of all tutors for certain acts in the administration of the goods of a minor. It was also because the *Corpus* could be bent in several directions that the Italian lawyers could offer their services to emperors as well as communal governments (more about this in Chapter 4).

Before moving on to the third hypothesis, a last problem in connection with democratic law should be mentioned, i.e. the role of Greek law. It is a question that has received little attention from the legal historians – the one conspicuous exception being Professor Troje – although it forms one of the most intriguing aspects of European legal history.[14] Perhaps it has received so little attention because it concerns something that has not played any part in that history, and historians are understandably more inclined to write about what happened than what did not. Nevertheless, the absence of persons or institutions in certain periods, if one comes to think about it, can be amazing and significant. The absence, certainly in the Middle Ages but to some extent afterwards also, of western interest in Greek law, and especially the law of the Athenian democracy, is most intriguing. Language was not a barrier, for Greek scientific and philosophical texts were made available in Latin translations from the Arabic and later directly from the originals. Nor was it for lack of interest in Greek thinking, on the contrary: western scholars in successive waves have been fascinated by the treasures of the Hellenic and Hellenistic past. The causes of this blind eye for Greek legal thought and practice are not easy to assess and deserve further research, but the following circumstances must have played a role.

There was no single collection in which the flower of Greek legal thought was brought together comparable to the *Corpus Juris* which made an inventory of all the best in Roman legal writing and was the starting point for the teaching of the glossators. Information on Greek law must be gathered from scattered rhetorical, historical and philosophical writings. The Romans were born soldiers and engineers, lawyers and administrators; in the intellectual field the law was their great legacy to the world. The Greeks certainly had interesting things to say about legal matters, and their experiments with democracy were highly remarkable, but their greatest contributions were elsewhere, in the arts and speculative thought.

Roman public law was useful to the rising monarchies of the later Middle Ages, because it was monocratic and authoritarian. It was also anti-feudal, not, of course, in the sense of a conscious attack on feudalism, which was unknown in Antiquity, but because its basic idea that all power derived from one central source was the antithesis of the dispersion of power over numerous centres, which was a conspicuous element of feudal society as it developed in Europe after the fall of the Frankish Empire. Roman law was a source of inspiration and a purveyor of ideas and arguments for modern states, each of which liked to proclaim itself 'an empire', as England did under Henry VIII.[15] The law of the Athenian democracy held no attraction for European monarchs.

The common law, essentially oligarchic and feudal, was incompatible with Roman law, but was equally incompatible with Greek democratic premises. It is not surprising therefore that England resisted the lure of Roman law, notably in the sixteenth and seventeenth centuries, when some royal sympathy for the civil law was noticeable and when the civilians tended to be royalist, as the common lawyers tended to be parliamentarians. Had Greek law been known in Europe, the Puritans might have derived some inspiration from it, but this was not the case.[16]

The links between Roman law and continental absolutism are clear, and have sometimes been demonstrated with brutal clarity, as when Duke Charles the Bold conquered the Prince-bishopric of Liège *manu militari* and abolished its old customs to replace them by Roman law.[17] It is not surprising therefore that the attack on the *ancien régime* in the eighteenth century went hand in hand with an attack on Roman law, and attempts to create an original modern law in the shape of the 'law of reason'. Again it is worthy of notice that Greek law was not thrown into the great intellectual battles of the time. Its tone was possibly too popular for the professors, top civil servants and enlightened monarchs who were responsible for the successes of natural law. It stands to reason that the monocratic papal Church, supported by sycophantic jurists who did not hesitate to write 'papa Deus est', was greatly in sympathy with, and supported by, the centralism and monocracy of the *Corpus Juris*. The government of the Church was the first to espouse civilian doctrine and to undergo the highest degree of romanisation. It fought against feudalism – the bitter Investiture Struggle was directed at the feudal order as it had grown up in the preceding two centuries – and there was nothing that could give it the slightest interest in the law of the Athenians: the monarchic element left no room for democracy, least of all the direct democracy of the agora.

EXPLANATIONS: POLITICAL HISTORY

Thus we come to the third hypothesis in the search for an explanation for the different impact on European law of judges, legislators and scholars. However, before building up a theory for Europe, it might be prudent to try one out for the two countries mentioned especially at the outset of this discussion, England and Germany. As far as these two countries are concerned, my view is that the prominent role of the judges in the former and of the jurists in the latter was a direct consequence of the political history and the different institutions of the two countries. In other words attention should be focused on the structure of the state and the foundations of public law, resulting from these countries' different histories, as the ultimate explanation of the contrasting role of their judges and law teachers.

I believe that the eminent role of German jurisprudence from about 1500 onwards was the consequence of the following circumstances. In the first place the lawgiver was weak, in a country without an effective national monarchy or parliament: after the death of Frederick II and the *Interregnum* the kingdom had dissolved and political life had shifted from the nation to a mosaic of principalities and free towns. The judiciary was also weak, as there was no generally recognised, guiding bench for the whole country (the first attempt came with the *Reichskammergericht* of 1495), but only a mosaic of regional or local benches, enjoying a limited authority. Some prestigious urban courts, such as the *Schöppenstuhl* of Magdeburg, enjoyed a great following in large areas, but never came anywhere near a national impact. This dual weakness, and the disparity of innumerable archaic and unwritten local customs led to the 'Reception' of the 'common written laws', in an attempt to modernise the law in one great leap forward. The direct and unavoidable consequence of the introduction of the *Corpus Juris* and its medieval accretions – a bulky body of learned books in Latin – was to hand over the law and its study and administration to the only ones who were trained to read, understand and explain Bartolus and Baldus, i.e. the cohort of learned lawyers with university degrees, led by the professors of Roman law: they henceforth held the key to legal science. It was fatal, for if the law is locked up in sacred books, it is the scholars who can read and understand them who are masters of the law; this was as true of Roman law and the civilians as of the Talmud and talmudic scholars. Established in the sixteenth, this situation lasted to the end of the nineteenth century.

Obversely I believe that the pre-eminence of English judges was the result of the following data. The law was not in the first place based on any one learned 'Holy Writ', hence it did not fall into the hands of a guild of scholarly jurists who had sole access to its bookish sources.[18] The central lawgiver, though a constitutional element to be reckoned with, often remained inactive. The legislation of even such a powerful king as Henry II is contained in a few printed pages of Stubbs's collection[19] and the first king since the Conquest to have a systematic legislative policy was Edward I; after him Parliament legislated in a haphazard way until the following great outburst under the Tudors. There was no comprehensive and continuous stream of legislation and, as is well known, the common law was firmly established before the days of Edward I. By contrast there was the strength and the continuity of the central courts, created by the monarchy, competent in first instance for a wide variety of cases arising over the whole kingdom. They acted with royal power behind them and were occupied by professionals who relentlessly continued to administer justice and to shape the law of the land even through the Wars of the Roses – in a regular stream of judgments. These royal judges, whose pronouncements were authoritative throughout the land, shaped the common law in co-operation with serjeants and barristers and were at the same time its guardians. In England the law was what the judge said it was, in modern Germany the law was what the professor said it was.

After this introductory glance at Germany and England, it might be interesting to pursue the hypothesis further and extend it to other major countries. This may refute or confirm the idea that the relative importance of judges, lawgivers and professors depended directly on the political history and the constitutional structure of their respective countries. Before undertaking this historical-comparative inquest, we might – by way of a *captatio benevolentiae* for lawyers who are not usually drawn to historical speculation – have a quick glance at the present-day powers of our trinity. Very briefly the picture is as follows.

The lawgiver is dominant and all powerful in socialist, totalitarian regimes, where learned jurists count for little and the judiciary has to look over its shoulder at what the party wants. In western Europe, outside England, the codes and laws are in principle predominant, but case law is far from negligible, the judges are independent, and the great jurists exercise considerable authority.

The judiciary plays a leading role in England. It is the land of precedents instead of codes and even in those fields which are now covered by legislation, the judges still exercise a considerable freedom of interpretation of statutes according to the old rules of construction and in the light of the fundamental principles of the common law and of reason. The reader should be reminded of what has already been said about the exclusion theory and the modern construction of statutes, in case he should be inclined to underrate the creative contribution of present-day English judges. Nor is the latter's invention limited to the construction of statutes. The most daring judges formulate theories which are based neither on statute nor on precedent and give protection to weak citizens purely on grounds of equity. A most striking example was offered by Lord Denning's notion of 'the married woman's equity', which allowed him to protect a deserted wife, who allegedly had an equity to remain in the house after the husband left her and could not be thrown out by building societies or banks or anyone else. This doctrine which, according to Lord Wilberforce, had no basis in law and was one of Lord Denning's 'great inventions', was run by the latter in the Court of Appeal for a number of years, until it came to the House of Lords, which had to reject it as long as the law was left unchanged by the legislature (which eventually changed the law in the sense of Lord Denning's ideas).[20] In the United States the role of the judges is paramount since they (and not only those of the Supreme Court) are the ultimate arbiters of the constitutionality of the laws.

The law faculties have little influence in socialist countries,[21] but jurists who are party functionaries can make themselves felt insofar as the party intervenes in the work of the judiciary. In the countries of what René David calls the 'Roman-Germanic family', the legal scholars, who are almost invariably professors (authors of multi-volume *Commentaires* or *Traités*, sometimes called 'élémentaire', which looks facetious on a work in ten volumes), exercise a potent influence on generations of students, barristers and judges. Some are also advisers in the *conseil d'état*, where the drafting of statutes is performed or controlled, and thus influence legislation in a direct way. In the common law countries the ideas, theories and books of learned jurists and professors are not so numerous or voluminous, and they have little influence on the legislature and even less on the senior judges. A recent study has shown that the Law Lords in England, the highest judicial authority in the United Kingdom, seldom read theoretical works or professional criticism of their judgments in the specialised journals; not a single Law Lord said that he wrote with academics in mind, nor do they interact on a regular basis with them. Hence it is not surprising that only two of the active Law Lords indicated that they had ever consulted or written to an academic when in doubt in a case; on the contrary, some Law Lords indicated that they did not pay much attention to academic comment in any event.[22] In the United States the fact that some judges are elected (though this is not the case with federal judges) may occasionally lead them, even when they are law graduates, to take more notice of popular reactions than of learned opinion. However, it is well known that the leading law schools are a factor of importance in America's legal development.

It may seem odd at first sight that both in England and the Soviet Union, which are otherwise miles apart, the law faculties have so little influence. The explanation must be that in England case law and in the Soviet Union codes and statutes are so paramount that neither leaves much room for the influence of jurists.

Let us add some historical depth to this picture and ask the same question not with the present day in mind, but the historical situation. The answers will be straightforward and familiar to every legal historian.

Judge-made law is a common-law tradition. It withstood the zeal of codifiers and modernisers of the nineteenth century.

Professor-made law was clearly predominant, as has already been pointed out, in northern Italy in the second

Middle Ages, in modern Germany from the sixteenth to the nineteenth century and in Holland from the days of Grotius to the introduction of the French codes.

Lawgivers' law was clearly predominant in revolutionary and nineteenth-century France. The same applies to Belgium in the nineteenth century and one of the most famous apostles of the Exegetical School, which dominated doctrine in France and Belgium, was a professor in the University of Ghent, François Laurent (died 1887). This School drew its name from the Greek term *exegesis* which means exposition and interpretation, in particular of the scriptures. The eponymous school was so called because it reduced legal teaching and writing to an exact and literal explanation of the text of the sacred Napoleonic codes. It is not surprising that the term 'exegesis', originally associated with bible studies, was applied to this School, since it believed in a limited number of holy books containing the law and nothing but the law. There was no law outside the codes and no law before it: the School was totally unhistoric. Professor Bugnet (died 1866) was heard to say that he did not teach civil law but only the Napoleonic code, as in the Middle Ages professors in the medical faculties did not teach anatomy but Galenus.[23] Not only did nothing exist before the codes, but nothing after them either. Napoleon had forbidden commentaries on them because these would soon take the place of his texts: hence all the faculty had to do was to provide a correct reading and precise understanding of the *ipsissima verba* of the codes. As to the judges, their creative contribution to the development of the law had been rudely curtailed or even eliminated, when the Revolution reduced them to the passive role of the famous '*bouches de la loi*', a sort of automata that produced the texts of the law applicable to any given case, merely repeating what the legislator had said. In certain phases the

Revolution had gone even further: not content with con-
demning the judges to a passive role, it attempted to get rid
of them altogether, especially of the appointed professionals. Judges were made elective and no qualification
was required. Furthermore it was hoped that the concilia-
tory phase, which was made obligatory, would eliminate
real litigation. This was a temporary aberration which was
ended by Napoleon, who reintroduced appointed and
professional judges.[24]

What caused this enthusiasm for lawgivers' law, shared
by revolutionary radicals, Napoleon and learned professors
of Laurent's sort? What motivated their aversion to ageless
custom, judge-made law and the creative role of jurisprudence? Factors of very different origins – some intellectual, some political – played their part. Legal science,
which for centuries had consisted of writings based on
Roman law, was bound to go out of favour as Roman law
itself came in for ever sharper criticism in the Age of
Enlightenment. The Humanists had unwittingly prepared
the ground by showing that Roman law, far from being a
timeless, God-given model for all nations and all periods,
was only the human product of a particular society at a
given period in history and had therefore no absolute,
'revealed' authority. Why, so the reasoning went in the
eighteenth century, should the law of an extinct civilisation
be the universal norm for modern Europe – the *moderni*
surpassed the *antiqui*! Modern Europe appealed to the
authority of something even more universal than the
Roman Empire, human reason itself, the basis of natural
law. The political reality also changed. In the Middle Ages
universalism, however unrealistic it may now seem, was
very much alive. The dream of a universal empire embrac-
ing all Christian nations was ever present in political
thinking, and even led Dante to write in favour of the

Roman-German Empire. In modern times, certainly after the treaties of Westphalia, that dream both of a universal Church and of a neo-Roman universal empire was dead. There was no power that encompassed, or could pretend or dream of encompassing, the peoples of Europe: national sovereignty had come to stay. But Roman law had nothing to offer these new nations. It knew no kingdoms, let alone sovereign nation states: it knew the universal empire and, on the local level, the *poleis* and the *municipia*. Therefore a law of nations had to be invented without Roman law, which is where natural law came in. It was initially a system of public international law, based on what seemed reasonable in a community of civilised nations. But the jurists who formulated this *Vernunftrecht*, and wrote most books about it, thought the best way of getting it introduced into real life was through legislation. Either legislation by enlightened monarchs, which most of them favoured, or legislation by revolutionary assemblies. Meanwhile, the 'law of reason' was in the eighteenth century a powerful tool against obscurantism, old-fashioned, Roman-law-based pedantry and all the evils of the *ancien régime*. The old social structure was criticised in the name of reason and eventually demolished. One has only to read the *cahiers de doléances* or the revolutionary codes of the last decade of the eighteenth century to be convinced. All this was natural enough – what is amazing is that this enormous enthusiasm for natural law gave way in the nineteenth century to silent disdain. The last thing Laurent wished to hear of was natural law – in which article of the *Code Civil* was that mentioned? The reasons for this sudden disgrace of natural law, which was brought about in a couple of years, merit special attention. They are not to be found in some new intellectual fashion, but in great social changes operated by the French Revolution and the regime of Napoleon.

Natural law had been the weapon of the eighteenth-century bourgeoisie against absolutism and its allies, the learned apostles of Roman law. But at the time of the great Napoleonic codes the bourgeoisie, having survived the storm of the Terror of 1792–94, obtained what it wanted: freedom of commerce, equality, the confiscation of Church lands and their entry into the market, and the rule of the legislator. Thus the great 'bourgeois peace' of the nineteenth century was established.[25] The last thing the new dominant class wanted was some fancy idea about a natural law which might endanger the codes. They were the firm legal foundations of the new world of entrepreneurs and financiers that flourished in the century of Louis Philippe, Napoleon III and Louis Adolphe Thiers. The 'law of reason' is the natural weapon of the dissatisfied and as the new burghers were satisfied and in power, they had no need for anything remotely seditious. On the contrary, a school of law that had no other ambition than the literal explanation of the sacrosanct codes was most welcome. Certainly, there was a new group of people in the nineteenth century, the industrial proletariat, and one might have expected them to look for help from natural law against the existing order. This did not happen and, on the Continent, many turned to the new, nineteenth-century ideology of marxism. What attracted them was, *inter alia*, the latter's frontal attack on property, something the eighteenth-century bourgeoisie had fought hard to safeguard, especially against the whims of autocracy. Also the natural-law philosophy was very static, whereas marxism, like hegelianism, was more in tune with the nineteenth century and its belief in dynamic evolution and dialectic, unending change.

Having surveyed the respective roles of case law, legislation and jurisprudence in a number of historic phases and countries, it is time to return to the third and principal hypothesis about the dominant factor behind them, the key to so much variety on the European scene. The discussion is limited to Europe from the twelfth century onwards, because in the 'first Middle Ages' the problem is irrelevant, as that was a primitive phase in which there was neither legislation nor jurisprudence and hardly any conserved case law. Everything was custom, very partially and occasionally put down in writing, and the story only begins when the crust of this primeval custom was broken by conscious efforts to push Europe forward among the civilisations which then existed around the Mediterranean Sea and along the Atlantic and North Sea coasts. I shall therefore take several leading countries and analyse the main lines of their legal history in order to see whether a political hypothesis is valid. The starting point is the dominant importance of the political situation in any given country: a strong unified state creates the conditions for a leading role to be played by a national legislator and powerful central courts, whereas whenever the state is discredited or weak, the absence of strong and prestigious legislative and judicial organs creates a vacuum that is filled by jurists, legal doctrine and professors of law.

England is the oldest unified nation-state or national monarchy in Europe, going back if not to the days of Alfred the Great, then certainly to the kings of the first half of the tenth century who reconquered the Danelaw. This Old-English state was the best administered in its time. When the national monarchies on the Continent were suffering in various degrees from the break-up of administration, which started at the end of the Carolingian period, the English monarchy built up a solid system of local government. It invented the royal writ, imitated on the Continent, and this writ ran throughout the country. The Normans took over

93

this solid monarchy with its nationwide impact. They added the military element of continental feudalism, but were able enough to prevent it from disrupting the country's unity. Henry II, the first Plantagenet king, was the founder of a corps of royal judges, who were competent in first instance for the whole country for a limited but expanding number of actions or writs. Their substantive law was feudal custom, their procedure was based on the writs and the jury. The law they, with the king himself, developed, became known as the common law of England, to distinguish it from local and regional customs, which continued to be applied by local courts. Before the end of Henry II's reign the first treatise on this common law and its courts, known as Glanvill, was written. Soon three distinct royal courts, all engaged in building up this new common law, were in operation, the Court of Common Pleas, fixed at Westminster,[26] the bench *coram rege*, travelling with the king and not fixed until the fourteenth century, and the Court of Exchequer, sitting at Westminster. Thus around 1200 a common law for the whole country was well established; the importance of this fact can best be realised if one remembers that France did not reach the stage of one code of laws for the whole realm until the years immediately following the Revolution of 1789. Once it was installed, the Court of Common Pleas never looked back, it sat in astounding continuity right down to the reforms of the nineteenth century and may be said to survive in the present-day High Court. This stability gave it extraordinary power, for it knew no ups and downs; as royal court it shared the prestige of the crown and could count on the might of the state for the execution of its judgments. It knew no rivals, although some courts arose to supplement its activities, either for good (the Court of Chancery) or temporarily (the Star Chamber, abolished under Cromwell). Round these judges, few but eminent, the Order of Serjeants at Law, a corporation of senior advocates, grew up, grouping the best legal brains, who were trained in the orbit of the central courts and from whose ranks the senior judges were recruited.[27] It was supported by impressive logistics, in the form of official enrolments and unofficial reports of cases. There was nothing like it in Europe; not even the Rota Romana was in any way comparable to it as far as its impact on the law was concerned.

England also had a great tradition of national legislation (the bench could not decide and create everything and judges always knew that adjudication and not legislation was their task), but it knew notable ups and downs and proceeded in fits and starts, unlike the majestic flow of the deliberations of the courts. One sign of the greatness of the Old-English monarchy is to be found in its impressive series of dooms, monuments of legislation or registration of existing rules, unique in Europe. However, after the catastrophe of 1066 this magnificent series came to an abrupt end. The Normans were no legislators, nor were the Plantagenets (in spite of some short texts under Henry II) and one has to wait, as has been seen, until the first ten years of 'the English Justinian', i.e. the years 1272–82, for a revival of the old tradition of national legislation. The parliaments of the Tudor age produced a considerable amount of important legislation, much of it originating with the royal government. In the eighteenth century a good deal passed through Parliament, but it was rather incoherent and the result of private members' initiatives: the government was not interested and was happy to let the courts develop important areas of law through the creation of precedents. The Reform of Parliament in 1832 changed all that and there arose, for about forty years, a body of coherent and important legislation that led to a great overhaul of English legal institutions which was inspired by the government. Legislative zeal cooled down around 1875 and was not revived until after the Second World War. For many centuries the idea dominated in legal circles that it was really best to leave the common law alone: statutes were not to be passed unless absolutely necessary and legislation was deemed too drastic a remedy. Adaptation was better than change and could be left to the courts, which were more able to deal with awkward precedents than one would think at first sight.[28] Lord Radcliffe, who played a leading role in the 1950s and 1960s, was outspoken about the need for the judge to act occasionally as a legislator, but advised that this should not be done too openly; he also expressed the view that 'getting round' an awkward precedent should not be beyond the intellectual possibility of a judge who really tried.[29] How loth some lawyers are to resort to legislation is amusingly highlighted by an anecdote reported by Roscoe Pound about a leader of the American bar who made provision in his will for a professorship in a law school, whose incumbent should teach the gospel of the futility of legislation:[30] it is not only English judges whose attitude 'is, at least in part and at times, caused by a certain mistrust and fear of statute law'.[31] The picture that emerges is basically one of the creation and development of the common law by powerful and ever-present royal courts, with legislation stepping in from time to time when something so drastic was required that it was really beyond the capacity of the judges.

This left little or no room for a class of professional jurists to exert their influence on the nation's life, and the tale of their impact on the law is therefore rather short. Glanvill, mentioned above, described the royal courts' practice which was grouped round a number of writs, mostly dealing with aspects of land tenure. The substance and the wording of his Latin treatise are thoroughly feudal and Anglo-Norman (much the same law had been growing up on both sides of the Channel, under a common prince). Here and there one hears a distant echo of Roman law, as if he was acquainted with some striking phrases of Justinian's *Institutes*; copies of the *Corpus* were available in England at the time, nor was civilian teaching unknown there and some Englishmen studied civil law on the Continent. Bracton's much larger treatise was in a different category. Not only had the number of available writs expanded but Bracton's analysis was also more detailed, and he made a conscious effort to link English development with the European currents of legal scholarship; in other words he was acquainted with Roman law, in particular Azo's *Summa Codicis*, and tried to fit it into what was by then a purely English and insular common law, since Normandy had been lost to the French crown and was gradually brought into line with French, Roman-inspired practice. Bracton's great attempt at a comprehensive theoretical exposition of the common law with the help of the *Corpus Juris* was important: it showed that the common law was reasonable and possessed internal coherence. However, it did not really fit the needs of the Profession, which was dominated by the practice of the courts and did not want theoretical *summae*, but information about cases, precedents and above all pleas, i.e. what the serjeants at law had proffered and what the judges had accepted or rejected, and why.

This could be found in the typical books of the following centuries, the Year-Books (and later the Law Reports). Judges and serjeants also needed to have the register of writs at hand, telling them what writs were available for what causes and how they worked. Whereas this *registrum brevium* followed the order of the writs, another influential, and intensely practical work, Littleton's *On Tenures*, consisted of the presentation of a great variety of land holdings, and the respective writs by which they were protected. Thus even there, where substantive law seemed to be the starting point, actions were seen to be essential. Right followed action and not the other way round.

The next ambitious attempt to present a coherent picture of English law was made in the *Reports* and *Institutes* of Sir Edward Coke, a series of works purporting to give a complete survey of English law. It was immensely erudite and full of precedents culled from medieval texts.[32] Coke reminds one of du Cange, a seventeenth-century French scholar who seems to have read every available scrap of medieval text – the work of several lifetimes of ordinary mortals – in order to extract information about the exact meaning of medieval Latin terms (the product of his zeal was an enormous dictionary of medieval Latin which he wrote single-handed).

In the *Commentaries* of Blackstone, the sun of the old common law, soon to be attacked, vilified and ridiculed by one of his pupils, Jeremy Bentham, shone in its final glory. Bentham wanted reform and codification, but he had no political leverage to bring them about. His pupil Brougham had friends in the right places and with him the great modernisation of England's judicial machinery began. Bentham had attacked the common law as 'mock law', 'sham law' and 'quasi-law' and had found the exercise of the judicial function an example of 'power everywhere arbitrary'. Some authors have tried to refute Bentham by pointing out that the system of precedent has produced a body of rules as determinate as any statutory rule and only liable to be altered by statute. However, this is not completely true since precedents have been known to be reversed and, less dramatically, to be circumvented by some fine distinction (see the remark of Lord Radcliffe quoted in note 29).[33] With Bentham, age and authority, judicial oracles or history carried no weight: only utility counted. He also cared for democracy, hence the demand that the law should be cognoscible and certain, i.e. codified.

Bentham was perhaps more a pamphleteer and agitator than a scholar. The most truly erudite jurist of the nineteenth century was John Austin (died 1859). He was an exceptional figure, not only as a theoretical jurist, but also because he was the first great lawyer in England since Bracton to be well acquainted with, and influenced by, continental doctrine: he studied in Germany and admired that country. There was not much that England could do with a theoretical lawyer in the first half of the nineteenth century: his doctrinal training had not prepared him for the bar, where he was unsuccessful. The only use the country could find for someone deeply interested in jurisprudence was a chair in a university and Austin not unnaturally became professor of Jurisprudence in London. However, hardly any students turned up for his abstractions and generalisations, so he gave up his chair – he was, after all, trying to revive the speculative study of law at a time when 'jurisprudence was a word which stunk in the nostrils of a practising barrister'[34] – and did some work on the Commission for the Modernisation of Criminal Law, where he was unhappy. It shows what little use society had for this learned jurist that nothing better could be found for him than a membership of a commission of enquiry into the state of Malta! Austin and his ideals could not have lived in a less appropriate time and place, for what he wanted was to turn legal studies into a science, emulating the universal validity of the study of the laws of physics. Like his friend Bentham, he believed in codification and rejected history as a dustbin of human follies; in other words he adored what the legal establishment most cordially detested, and detested what they most deeply revered. In the present century the general reverence for the judiciary was even encouraged by the academic lawyers, whose task it should be to examine the trend of case law with scholarly criticism. Sir William S. Holdsworth (died 1944), famous jurist and legal historian, felt, for example, that 'the law teacher ought not to encourage criticisms of the judiciary in an age of scepticism'.[35] If it is possible to discuss seriously whether English lawyers 'place the courts at the centre of their legal universe', or accept that Parliament is 'the real sun around which the law revolves',[36] nobody would put jurisprudence anywhere near the centre – a pale moon, reflecting the wisdom of the bench might be its appropriate place in this cosmology.

No greater contrast could be imagined than that between the English and the Italian development. In the latter, well into the nineteenth century, there was a total lack of political unity. In the south there was a feudal kingdom, in the centre the papal state and in the north the *regnum Italiae*, ruled by the Roman emperor-German king and incorporated in his empire. However, royal authority was combated there from the second half of the eleventh century onwards, and at the latest after the death of Frederick II (died 1250) even the fiction or the dream of an effective monarchical rule was given up. Northern Italy was to all intents and purposes divided into a number of urban republics, which slowly developed into modern principalities under the sway of rulers of the type of Machiavelli's *Principe*. The consequences for the legal life of the country were foreseeable: no central high court of justice, which could have developed a national law. Only local and regional courts, without real prestige (except possibly the Court at Naples for southern Italy) or the logistical means to build up a great tradition of case law existed. There was, of course, no question of a national lawgiver: legislation was purely local or at best provincial, with the ephemeral significance of provincial institutions devoid of real prestige or power, subjected to the petty power-game of local notables. Legislation there was in abundance but it was occasional, changeable and devoid of real interest. The vacuum caused by this state of affairs was filled by the learned lawyers, trained in the study of the *Corpus Juris*, which dwarfed the native law books by its sheer quality. Soon these jurists were drawn into litigation, where their science and the prestige of their imperial law were solid weapons. They were also called upon to harmonise local statutes or to devise a doctrine for the conflicts between them – the origin of modern international private law. One of their main occupations became the counselling of local courts, and collections of these *consilia* circulated and were widely quoted. Thus the general picture was the antithesis of England: the role of the professors, imbued with Roman and medio-Roman law, was all pervading, while case law and legislation were of negligible importance.[37]

In Germany too the political picture was that of a very divided country. There also unity failed to be established – or rather re-established – until the second half of the nineteenth century and there also the break-up was final after the death of Frederick II. Although a nominal and symbolic figurehead of the 'Germanies' continued to be recognised, political life had withdrawn to the ecclesiastical and lay principalities and the imperial and free cities. The consequences are easy to guess: absence of a central bench with a truly national impact, but a pleiad of local and regional courts, which sometimes managed to enjoy a real prestige, but never outside certain regional boundaries. There was, with the possible exception of a series of

Landfrieden, no central legislation: local custom was paramount and seldom put in writing, let alone promulgated
with the force of law. A great attempt to overcome these
deficiencies was made in the heady days of European
Humanism as part of Emperor Maximilian's efforts to
recreate some unity in Germany. This entailed both
abolishing medieval customs, in order to put in their place,
as the new law of the kingdom, 'the common written laws'
– Roman and canon law – and the foundation, in 1495, of
the Court of the Imperial Chamber or *Reichskammergericht* as the creation not of the emperor, but of the empire
and its estates. The aim was to form a court of appeal for
the whole country and to watch over the application of the
new learned law. Originally the court consisted half of
learned jurists and half of knights, but by the middle of the
sixteenth century all were to be jurists. The victory of
Roman law was real, although not absolute: local traditions, particularly in Saxony, put up a staunch resistance.
The success of the new High Court of Justice was less
satisfactory: the jealousy of various principalities was such
that they obtained exemption from its jurisdiction by
securing privileges *de non appellando* and *de non evocando.* Nevertheless, the victory of the *Corpus Juris* caused
the breakthrough of the professors who taught and
explained it, of the barristers who quoted from it and of the
local registrars or pensionaries who had obtained a law
degree and advised the local courts (which were largely
occupied by non-jurists) what line of the *Corpus* should be
applied and which doctor's opinion – Bartolus's or Baldus's
– should be preferred.

The great codes of the Enlightenment, although inspired
by the lofty ideas of the School of Natural Law, very often
had to rely on the old trusted Roman law when it came to
the detailed rules, particularly in matters of contract. Hence

they in fact, although not in theory, kept a good deal of Roman law alive and the postponement of a pure German civil code till 1900 meant that throughout the nineteenth century Roman law and its high priests kept the upper hand. As a truly national parliament and a truly national High Court did not arise before the unification in the days of Bismarck, the jurists dominated legal life for four centuries, even to the point, as we have seen, of telling the judges what sentences to give.

The Republic of the United Provinces was, as the name indicates, a federal state and, as federal states go, it belonged to the weaker type, i.e. the federal organs were not very developed or powerful – something the United States consciously avoided when it drafted its own constitution. The central political organ *par excellence*, the Estates General, far from being a truly national parliament, was no more than a meeting of the deputies from the provincial estates, where real power lay. In these circumstances it was only normal that there was neither central legislation for the whole republic (and little in the separate provinces), nor any 'homologation' of the old customs at the command of the central government. Of course, there could be no central court of appeal either. The High Court of Holland and Zealand had a certain prestige – and only then because Holland and Zealand were by far the richest and most influential regions – outside these two provinces, but no legal authority. In these circumstances Hugo Grotius founded Roman-Dutch law, which gained a great following and, since it was mostly based on Roman law, gave the learned jurists a clear advantage over all other elements in the legal life of the Republic. This was one of the reasons why Dutch jurists and Dutch universities had a European audience and played such a considerable and original part in the rise of modern jurisprudence. All this gave Dutch law a distinctly learned flavour, with a high degree of attention to theory and speculation, which it has conserved to the present day, in spite of the Napoleonic codifications which were introduced.

France became a unitary nation-state long before Germany and Italy, but long after England. This time-lag was caused by the collapse of the French monarchy in the tenth and eleventh centuries, when the Old-English state was organising itself. The kingdom of France was divided into autonomous principalities and, in a second wave of decomposition, into castellanies: micro-states with diameters of between five and ten kilometres, grouped round a feudal overlord and his castle. The reaction started in the twelfth century (when the English King Henry II ruled over more French land than the king of France) and in some four centuries the monarchy established political unity in the old western part of Charlemagne's realm. The emergence of a strong monarchy led, around the middle of the thirteenth century, to the establishment of a central royal court, the Parlement of Paris, with jurisdiction over all France. This court enjoyed great power and prestige and its members were professionals who had university degrees in Roman law. It was, however, rather different from the English central courts in that it was mainly a court of appeal and exercised no jurisdiction in first instance, except over certain important persons and matters. Also it had to apply the customs of the region whence the appeals came so that, although it exercised some unifying influence, it did not produce a common law for the whole kingdom. Legally, the kingdom remained divided, for whereas in the southern part, roughly about one third of the country, Bolognese law quickly took the place of the old Roman customary law, in the northern two-thirds local customs of Germanic and feudal origin prevailed. The revitalised monarch of the twelfth century became aware, albeit very tentatively, of its legislative duties and royal legislation never disappeared again during the following centuries. It was not so extensive as its English counterpart, at least during the Middle Ages, but became important from the sixteenth century onwards and especially under Louis XIV and Louis XV: parts of their *ordonnances* passed into Napoleon's codes. In contrast with England, French legislation remained the responsibility of the king and his collaborators, not the national representative assemblies or *Etats généraux*. The lack of legal unity also meant that, even as late as the eighteenth century, some important ordinances could not be given validity for the whole country: there were separate ordinances on wills, for example, for the north and the south in 1735. Finally the French monarchy, from the mid-fifteenth century onwards, put a royal stamp on the division of the country by ordering the 'homologation' (i.e. the recording and promulgating as law) of numerous local customs. This 'homologation' was a strange phenomenon, a hybrid, for on the one hand it was customary law registered and fixed in writing, but on the other legislation, for those texts were given force of law and no other customary rule could prevail against them. The 'homologated' customs had in fact lost some of the essential characteristics of customs, i.e. that they live in people's consciousness, come and go and evolve with changing ways of life and modes of thought: custom is flexible, the written text of a 'custom' issued as the sole law is not.[38] Legal science in those circumstances stood a good chance. Legislation was never so comprehensive as to dispense with what the jurists had to say (that would only come with the codes and the Exegetic School), and the Parlements, that of Paris and its provincial off-shoots, far from developing a common law, had to administer various customs. Nevertheless the members of those

Parlements had all been trained by studying Roman law –
no customary law was taught in the universities until the
seventeenth century – and some of this learning inevitably
rubbed off on the law of the land. Furthermore, the authors
who, from the thirteenth century onwards, wrote expositions of, and commentaries on, various regional customs
were scholars who had learned their trade in the school of
Roman law and again, the method, the terminology and
even some of the substance of Roman law rubbed off on
their *coutumiers*. There was therefore ample scope for
learned jurists in France.

In the south, where Germanic occupation had been thin
and a Roman law of sorts had always lived on, the seed of
Bologna fell on fertile soil and civilian professors and
universities already flourished in the twelfth century. In the
thirteenth, when Orleans started on its illustrious career as
a law university of international repute, professors such as
Pierre de Belleperche and Jacques de Revigny were no mere
epigones of the Italian glossators, but made an original
contribution to the study of Roman law, and French jurists
played a major role in the humanist movement, Cujas being
the greatest among them.

From the thirteenth century onwards in the north there
was a continuous stream of learned jurists who wrote
commentaries on customary law, using the tools of the
Roman law schools, whose *alumni* they were. Nevertheless,
unlike in Germany, there was no wholesale 'reception' of
Roman law in France. This may seem surprising, considering the fact that it would only have meant extending to the
whole of France a system that already prevailed in the
south. The resistance to Roman law, led by such luminaries
as Charles Dumoulin, was politically inspired. Roman law
was felt to be imperial law (*Kaiserrecht*) and imperial law
meant the law of Germany and of the Emperor Charles V,

who was almost constantly at war with France. To build up a truly national law, using French customs and particularly that of Paris as a starting point, was felt to be a more dignified solution. The overall impression is of a country where neither judiciary, nor legislature nor scholars enjoyed a clear cut preponderance, but all three contributed in equal measure. This tallied with political reality. The French monarchy was strong enough to found the Parlement of Paris and to adopt Roman-canonical procedure, but not nearly strong enough to impose one common law for the whole country. Again, this monarchy was forceful enough to produce a good deal of legislation, but not to overrule local customs, which were even given official status, thus preserving legal diversity. There were national representative assemblies, but because of strong local political traditions they were powerful only in times of weakness of the crown, so that they could not develop into a national lawgiver. The defence of the country's freedoms did not lie in the hands of the *Etats généraux*, but of the Parlements, which often and obstinately resisted new royal legislation.[39] The schools on the other hand, having to compete with powerful Parlements and active royal legislators, could never dominate the scene. Nevertheless they were a force in the land. They taught the Roman law that became the norm in southern France and were the teachers of the judges even in the north. They also gave authoritative interpretations of the official *coutumes* and subjected them to such cogent criticism that the government issued, for example, a revised edition of the Custom of Paris after Charles Dumoulin had criticised the first version. From Dumoulin to Pothier a line of great jurists, familiar with customary and Roman law and with royal legislation, was striving towards a valid system of law for the whole of France, the *droit commun français*: doctrine achieved what legislation could not. The quality of their work explains their influence, even outside French frontiers: Pothier was quoted by Blackstone and by nineteenth-century English judges.

The state of equilibrium which has been described prevailed, of course, only until 1789. The Revolution disturbed it deeply, by placing statutes and codes at the absolute pinnacle, reducing the judges to a secondary role and simply abolishing the law faculties. Blind veneration for the law and even the letter of the law dominated the nineteenth century. The twentieth has seen the return to a better equilibrium: the codes still prevail on principle, but the courts enjoy a freedom of interpretation unheard of in the previous century. Professors also have become more daring in their teaching and take into account not only the letter of the law, but its sense and the social necessities of the age.

After this rapid survey of five countries it seems justifiable to conclude that the political development of the various European nations was largely responsible for the respective importance of the judiciary, the legislature and the law faculties in the shaping of the law. This implies that legal history is part of political history and poses the question of how it accords with the more traditional view that 'legal history is part of cultural history'.[40] Whether legal history is concerned with the development of ideas or the clash of interests has been a moot point for generations[41] and cannot be entered into here, even summarily. Nobody, of course, maintains that the general cultural atmosphere has left legal development untouched, nor does anyone believe that the rise of monarchy, aristocracy or democracy made no impact on the lawyers and their books. Nevertheless, some historians believe that the power-struggle is paramount and that lawyers are forced to think within a framework established by extraneous events, while others maintain that the rise and refinement of legal concepts are an autonomous flow that majestically goes on along lines of their own intellectual perfection taking little notice of the great political upheavals and their clamouring protagonists. All I hope for is that these observations throw some new light on the historic impact of political and institutional factors on European legal development.

There remains, however, one legal system to be mentioned – not of a country but of a corporation – canon law. How do the law and the constitution of the Church fit in with this hypothesis? It will soon become clear that the Church is a very interesting case *sui generis*. For in the Church – and one is thinking here of the great formative period of the canon law, from Gratian (*c.* 1140) to Boniface VIII (died 1303) – the role of legal science and the jurist was paramount, although there was a strong central authority vested in the pope, who was a great and continuous source of legislation. Numerous constitutions and, above all, thousands of decretals issued from the Lateran Palace to uphold and develop the law of the Church, a model of organisation for many states. This same pope and his curia, later the Rota Romana, were also the supreme judges: thousands of cases went to Rome, some in first instance but most in appeal, to be judged there or committed to papal judges delegate in their countries of origin. And yet there can be no doubt that the faculties of canon law played a very great role in the development of ecclesiastical law to a science and that their commentaries on canons and decretals were authoritative. In addition the court held by the bishop's official (who was always a university graduate) became, from about 1200 onwards, the normal place for handling litigation in first instance. How then could jurists be so important in a society where central authority –

lawgiver and judge – was preponderant? The idea that the jurist's importance is universally related to the weakness of the central authority does not seem to be valid here. This is indeed so, for the simple reason that in the Church the central lawgiver and the learned jurist were one and the same person. From Alexander III onwards throughout the classic age of canon law, great papal lawgivers – Alexander III, Innocent III, Innocent IV, Boniface VIII – were also great jurists. The Church was the one society where scholars became rulers: no medieval king, however intelligent, was a university graduate, but numerous popes were and the great lawgivers especially had obtained their degrees in law at a university and written authoritative commentaries or *summae* on canon law before obtaining the papal tiara. In no other society did bright law graduates become supreme: they might become the councillors of rulers, the assistants of lawgivers – like the famous legists around Philip IV the Fair – but they did not become crowned heads. In the Church scholars acquired power, fulfilling in a way the platonic ideal of the philosopher-king. The reason, of course, is that the Church is no nation-state, although the similarities in administration, adjudication, legislation and fiscal organisation might lead one to forget this. The power structure of the Church is not based on a territory and feudal land, but on religion, as defined and revealed in the Holy Books. It is a community of believers held together by faith, not of inhabitants of a particular territory, even though much of its public law came from the Roman Empire, the greatest state the world had ever seen. The raison d'être of the Church, whatever the techniques of its organisation, are the Holy Books and their religion, even though there were periods when administration seemed to oust theology. Hence the role of scholars, who understand the holy precepts, is bound to be important: they hold the key of the meaning of Holy Writ. This is valid in the first place for theologians, but also for lawyers, for the Holy Books contain norms of behaviour as well as truths. The particular role of the papal lawgiver originated with the Gregorian reform and the rise of the papal theocracy: since the reforming papacy had the ambition to transform Christianity, popes had to be great legislators. Gregory VII found many practices – malpractices in his eyes – which had been established by custom, and the only way to attack custom is to legislate: i.e. to abolish 'bad customs' and issue new rules. Thus Gregory's distrust of custom. But custom often appears in the form of case law, hence the weak role of the latter in the classic period of the twelfth and thirteenth centuries. Justinian's rule 'legibus, non exemplis judicandum est'[42] served that period very well. This explains the remarkable fact that although there was very extensive judicial activity in Rome and in the courts of archbishops and bishops, case law in the form of collections of judgments was of secondary importance. It is only at a late stage that the systematic collection and publication of the sentences of the Rota Romana got under way.[43] The classical period of the canon law was the era of the jurists-lawgivers, the scholars on the throne. Formally speaking their constitutions and decretals were legislative acts, but their substance was the doctrine of the schools: it was scholars' law, based on the teaching of the universities, where the future popes had been students and professors. This regime of the professorial lawgiver was unique in Europe – the nearest equivalent would be certain lawyer-dominated modern parliaments from the American and French revolutions onwards.

3

THE DIVERGENT PATHS OF COMMON
LAW AND CIVIL LAW

Having established in a broad comparative survey what
caused the preponderance of judge, legislator or jurist in
Europe, I now intend to return to my starting point, the
difference between the English common law and the rest of
Europe. The reason why the English judiciary played such
an exceptional role has been established, but this fact does
not by itself explain why the English common law is so
different. One can very well imagine an English, judge-
made variant of a common European law. Thus one hears
that at the present time the same European Community
rules are not interpreted similarly on the Continent and in
the United Kingdom. Judges' law in one country and
legislators' law in others would normally have produced
some differences, but these might have been technical only,
without involving the substance of the law. To put it in
more concrete terms: one can imagine a situation where the
substance of European feudal law remained common to all
countries, even if its development in the course of the later
Middle Ages was the task of the judiciary in some countries
and of the legislature in others. Equally one can imagine
that more progressive laws corresponding to an urban and
commercial society would have arisen through the action of
judges in some countries and of kings and estates in others.
The difference between common law and continental law
goes much further than that: they were not only developed
by different organs, their very substance was different, the

one being traditional, native and feudal, the other new, foreign and Roman. A legal system based on feudal principles, albeit adapted and modernised in the course of the centuries, and a legal system based on the very unfeudal doctrines and principles of Roman and neo-Roman law are worlds apart, not only in their various techniques in lawmaking, but in their very foundations. And it is to the exact historic circumstances in which this divergence originated that attention will now be turned.

COMMON LAW AND CIVIL LAW: THE PARTING OF THE WAYS

Right through the early Middle Ages and up to the mid-twelfth century English and continental law belonged recognisably to one legal family, Germanic and feudal in substance and in procedure. Except for possible linguistic complications, a traveller from the Continent in the days of King Stephen would have had no problem in recognising the rules, arguments and modes of proof in an English manorial, borough or feudal court. A century later the landscape had changed: Roman law and Roman-canonical procedure were transforming life in many parts of the Continent (and others were to follow), whereas in England a native law, common to the whole kingdom, that was – and remained – free from the substance and the procedure of the new continental fashion, had arisen. The moment when this dichotomy arose can be pinpointed exactly. It was in the reign of King Henry II, when certain reforms in judicial organisation and procedure were carried out which modernised English law before Roman law entered the scene with such wide and immediate success that no need was felt in later centuries, when the neo-Roman model was available, to give up the native system. The main changes of

King Henry II's reign were the foundation of one group of royal judges with competence in first instance for the whole kingdom to settle litigation of certain types on land (which meant feudal litigation), and the introduction of the jury in civil and in criminal cases as the standard mode of proof (instead of ordeals and judicial combat). Litigants flocked to these new courts and their new procedures – and paid for the privilege of being heard there – and the judges built up a common feudal law. Their role was expanded by the creation of new writs, bringing ever more types of cases before them. The old local courts were sadly left behind, not because of any law or crafty scheme on behalf of the king, but because of the quality of justice that was dispensed by his judges. It should never be forgotten that this important innovation was not a solely or typically English event, it was, in more than one sense, Anglo-Norman. Henry II introduced the new scheme of writs and juries in his Norman duchy as well as in his English kingdom; the feudal law administered in the ducal and royal courts – at Rouen and at Westminster – was the same and the judges belonged to one and the same class of French-speaking knights, who often possessed at the same time their old family lands in Normandy and their newly-acquired lands in England (all feudally held directly or indirectly from the same king-duke, Henry II Plantagenet). It was the conquest of Normandy by the French monarchy and the gradual introduction of Roman-inspired French law into the duchy that turned Anglo-Norman into purely English law. What became the English common law started as Anglo-Norman law, shared by a kingdom and a duchy that were not separated but united by the Channel: what came to be the hallmark of insularity was initially not insular at all.

The reasons for this remarkable development under King Henry are not far to seek. It was not to some stubborn trait of the English character or the 'national spirit' that one must look – the new system was not English anyway, but Anglo-Norman and even more Norman than English – but to specific historical circumstances. Henry II was an exceptionally powerful monarch, accepted by all, 'French and English', and feudalism was firmly under royal control; even the Church felt the strong impact of the crown, although it put up a fierce fight for its privileges. England was prosperous enough to afford a relatively large body of professional central judges. The royal court responded also to an undeniable feeling of dissatisfaction with the existing state of affairs. The local courts were dispersed and often weak: every lord who had a few vassals could hold his court, but what could it undertake against a rebel, how could it enforce its judgments? In particular the protection of the possession of land – the livelihood of almost everybody in twelfth-century England – was inadequate. There was doubt about various customs and there could be confusion between the Old-English and the recent Norman rules. The prosecution of crime was inadequate and largely in the hands of individuals, and various experiments were tried to remedy this state of affairs. And last but not least, there was dissatisfaction with the existing, archaic modes of proof, which were as hazardous as they were harmful (if they were not fatal). Strong, quick and efficacious remedies offered by the king and his judges seemed to be the only solution (as in the nineteenth and twentieth centuries, wide state intervention seemed to many the only remedy for the unfortunate results of unbridled capitalism). Only the central government could cope with the situation, but what could it turn to? Not to Roman law and Roman-canonical procedure, for which it was too early, as not even the Church courts had switched over to the new style in King Henry's days. The schools were still busy working out the first steps of what, in later centuries, was to lead to a triumphal conquest of the Continent. No legal 'transplant' could be of any help here, therefore using and reshaping existing material into something new and adequate was the only answer. This meant the judicialisation of the royal writs, especially those for the protection of possession of land, so that people could count on their next harvest. This meant also the systematic use of the jury, which had previously been resorted to occasionally in a variety of circumstances. It finally meant the creation of a central body of royal justices, fixed at some certain place. Thus a modernised and for that time satisfactory judiciary and body of law came into existence, free of Roman law influence.

On the Continent at this juncture the main modernisation of the law was taking place in the urban world, particularly in northern Italy and Flanders, where local courts of aldermen were granted liberty to use progressive procedures and rules. Nowhere did these dispersed efforts lead to new, unified, national or even regional law. The Church courts, manned henceforth by the learned bishops' officials, began to apply the new law from the Bolognese textbooks around 1200. About the middle of the thirteenth century the kingdoms began to follow suit (Sicily being, however, ahead of the others).[1] Gradually, under the influence of the universities and following the example of the ecclesiastical courts, Roman law was transforming continental civil and to some extent criminal law, with the active help of governments. But it was the universities that created the new and modern, as opposed to the archaic and feudal law; they provided the books and the men who alone could bring about this new departure on the Continent. In Italy (north and south), southern France and eastern Spain – old Mediterranean lands – this new Roman law was already firmly entrenched in the thirteenth century. In northern France, Germanic and feudal custom resisted, particularly since it produced some original modernisation of its own, but even there in the thirteenth century the commentators of customary laws were already working with Roman law as their system of reference: they were familiar with its vocabulary, it provided their grammar and it was the universal treasure house where customary lawyers could find answers to the questions left unanswered by local usage. Gradually the courts were manned by people with university degrees. Germany resisted the spread of the civil law even longer, but when it gave in, it went much further than France and 'received' the 'common written laws' *in toto*. During the crucial thirteenth and fourteenth centuries, the English common law was safely and firmly embedded in national life. It had its own courts, occupied by the best lawyers in the country. It had its Glanvill and its Bracton, comprehensive expositions which presented the common law as a self-sufficient and reasonable whole, its registers of writs, some of which were official texts, its bar and the serjeants at law, a well established and self-assured corporation from whose ranks the senior justices were appointed, and its Year Books, with up-to-date reports of what happened in the courts. Its practitioners were conscious of its distinctness and, insofar as they ever looked across the Channel, were convinced of its superiority, as is clear in John Fortescue's *De laudibus legum Angliae* of *c.* 1470, which made a comparison between English and French law, much to the detriment of the latter. Even as early as the thirteenth century, English common law had embarked on an expansionist offensive of its own – a minor foretaste of its worldwide impact in later centuries.[2] Lastly, and this was probably the most important consideration, the common law was the safeguard of lawful landholding and therefore the cornerstone of every fortune of every notable family and every church in the country. Power and prestige were based on land, and the safety of the land was based on the common law.

THE WAYS REMAIN SEPARATE

If the reason why the common law was so different in its initial stages is understandable, the question next arises why it conserved its distinct character right through the centuries, down to the present time. That it protected landed wealth is not in itself a sufficient explanation, for on the Continent this was not strong enough to prevent the progress of Roman law: an absolutist state bent on reducing feudalism and using Roman law was quite capable of gaining the day, even against the old feudal class.

English law was not so distinct that it could not have taken over Roman law at some later stage. Scotland at first followed the English common law, which in the course of the thirteenth century seemed to be taking deep roots in Scottish soil, to be abandoned only in the fourteenth century and replaced in the sixteenth by Roman law of continental origin. So European unity eventually might have been restored and English and continental law might have ended on the same wavelength. It cannot seriously be suggested that anyone on the Continent thought of taking over the English common law, even though some elements, such as the jury, were imitated in the eighteenth and nineteenth centuries. But in the Middle Ages the English jury was a main stumbling-block for lawyers on the Continent. Churchmen there in the thirteenth century rejected the idea of the jury, which left the decisive verdict in a law case in the power of a dozen illiterate rustics, as utterly ridiculous and absurd. The tone had been set by a decretal of Pope Innocent III, who wrote in 1199 to the bishop of Poitiers that it had come to his attention that in the said diocese an unreasonable (*minus rationabilis*) custom was observed, i.e. that after the hearing of the allegations of the parties all persons present, whether literate or illiterate, wise or unwise, were asked what the law was, so that whatever they or some of them said was taken as judgment.[3]

If the possibility of continental borrowing from English law was slight, the occasions for the penetration of civilian influence in England were serious and numerous. Roman law and Roman-canonical procedure made their influence felt if not in the common-law courts then in other courts, such as those of the Church. Ever since the famous controversy between Stubbs and Maitland, nearly a century ago, it has been known that English, medieval, ecclesiastical courts followed the law of the Roman Church just like other countries of Latin Christendom (which did not exclude the formation of local customs and variants). How fully and how early the English courts took on the new learned model was demonstrated with particular clarity and rich detail in the recent edition of cases from the courts in the Province of Canterbury in the thirteenth century.[4] The Church courts provided a continuous and different example of handling litigation.

In the Court of Chancery the chancellor exercised his equitable jurisdiction, as a correction of, or complement to, the harshness or deficiencies of the common-law courts. Indeed, Chancery offered remedies which were a matter of course in the professional procedure, but not available in the common-law courts, such as injunction, specific performance and rectification of documents. Since the chancellor was almost always a bishop whose court had arisen long after the new Roman-canonical process was established, it is not surprising that its procedure was much closer to that of the Church than of the common law – the jury was a notable absentee and the interrogation of witnesses on 'articles' one of the most striking loans from the *ordines judiciarii*. The Court of Admiralty, which left regular records from 1524 onwards, followed a procedure of the civilian type and administered a commercial and maritime law that was cosmopolitan rather than English and familiar with various forms of business unknown to the common law. The Star Chamber also proceeded more forcefully and intervened more directly in the course of litigation than did the common law: it was extremely active and popular, *inter alia*, because it did not suffer from the rigged and intimidated juries which were the bane of the time. Not only could these un-common-law-like moves be observed by everyone interested in the law, but the theory of civil and canon law was being taught in the two English universities as in so many others on the Continent and in Scotland. And, of course, those Englishmen who found that their own universities did not quench their thirst for knowledge could and did go to study abroad.

The high tide in the fortunes of Roman law, with a 'reception' in Germany and Scotland and a much-debated possibility of a 'reception' in France, was in the sixteenth century. It is not surprising therefore that in England also various circles showed an earnest desire for the cobwebs of the medieval law to be swept away and Roman law – 'common to all civilised Europe' – to be introduced in their stead. Such, naturally enough, was the opinion of some scholars who had studied on the Continent, but it was also the opinion of certain people in authority. The foundation of regius chairs of civil law by King Henry VIII is witness to it. This monarch had great respect for everything imperial, notably the law of imperial Rome, and also the great

Christian emperors of Rome, in whose line of monarchs he saw himself – England being his 'Empire'.[5] The 'danger' to the common law in those heady Renaissance days has been exaggerated and its power of internal renewal underrated, so that scholarly opinion does not now hold that the common law was ever in real peril.[6]

The events of the seventeenth century were, of course, closely linked with the political drama of the Stuart monarchy. Common law and common lawyers were identified with the Parliamentary cause, although not all judges in the common-law courts always stood against the kings, and a famous lawyer like Sir Matthew Hale had very positive things to say about Roman law and lamented that the Digest was so little studied in England.[7] Roman law and the prerogative courts were identified with absolutism and so quite naturally were the civilians. The victory of the parliamentary party gave the latter no chance: the Puritans were certainly not in favour of Roman law, whose very name reminded them of popery (it would not be surprising if Stubbs's attack on Roman law, which was mentioned above, was somehow caused by an unconscious linking of Roman law with the Roman Church, the inquisitorial enemy of religious freedom).[8]

It is appropriate to pause here for a moment and to see what John Selden (died 1654), lawyer, legal historian and active member of the Parliamentary party, thought about the contacts between civil and canon law. He entered into this question in a dissertation which presents itself as an essay on *Fleta*, a medieval law book, but which is in fact an early history of the 'reception' of Roman law in medieval and early modern Europe. He devotes chapter 9 to an analysis of the English aversion from the use of Roman law. He gives two reasons why civil law had no greater effect in its use by English lawyers. One is 'the unconcealed aversion

The ways remain separate

which our ancestors had to it so far as it concerns principles of government' (*regimen publicum*); the other is 'the remarkable esteem in which the English or common law was held and our constant faithfulness to it as something immemorially fitted to the genius of the nation' ('*gentis hujus genio ab intima antiquitate adaptata*').[9] It is noteworthy that Selden here uses the expression 'genius of the nation' long before it became popular in Europe around 1800. However, it is not so strange that the national spirit should have been invoked so early by an English historian, since the common law was obviously the most idiosyncratic and purely national legal system of all Europe.

In the eighteenth century Roman law was coming under growing criticism on the Continent itself, so it certainly was not going to conquer England. On the contrary, this was the time of continental anglomania and attempts to borrow from English law and institutions. Nor were things different in the nineteenth century. There was the occasional reference to Roman law in an English judgment, but it was always accompanied by the proviso that this was not a reference to a system that had any force of law in England.[10] In this period of Britain's greatest glory part of her pride and self-confidence was faith in the excellence of her legal system, deemed superior to all others, as Britain itself was superior to all powers in the world. It is not surprising therefore that little notice was taken in England of the teaching of the German Pandectists. Some learned authors attribute this to deliberate attempts on the part of English lawyers to keep their system obscure and to block attempts at rationalising it. Thus we read in an authoritative German work: 'In England the teaching of the Pandectists had very little effect. This is hardly surprising since England had always denied admission of Roman institutions and methods: English lawyers, if only to secure their

123

professional monopoly by keeping the law obscure, blocked any attempts to rationalise the concepts and structure of their law.'[11] Have the doctors of civil law always written such luminous works in a limpid and enjoyable prose for the general reader, and would one expect to find the tomes of Windscheid's *Pandektenrecht* in the hands of the man in the street, keen on breaking the monopoly of the legal profession?

WHICH DIVERGED FROM WHICH?

When one thinks of a divergence between common law and civil law, one is naturally inclined to see the former as diverging from the latter, which – one assumes – represented the mainstream in European legal history. Many lawyers and historians, particularly, of course, on the Continent of Europe, when faced with the question who diverged from whom, will find it obvious that if one country took an un-Roman path as against ten or fifteen others, it is the one which diverged (or should one say deviated?) and not the ten or fifteen others. Viewed in a strictly European context this seems indeed a normal reaction, but things look altogether different if one considers not European but universal legal history: in that light it is the continental development that appears odd and the English normal. Indeed, the two main features of continental law – that it was based on one authoritative *corpus juris* and that it is codified – clearly constitute two anomalies, which may really be reduced to one, the fact that continental law is based on a 'sacred text'. The veneration enjoyed by the great modern codes – certainly until the end of the nineteenth century – is comparable to that for the *Corpus* in the Middle Ages, and there is little difference between the literal explanation of the one by the glossators and the verbatim scrutiny of the others by the professors of the Exegetical School. The Romans themselves, the great teachers of the continentals, knew nothing like our modern codes. Their law was developed piecemeal in the course of centuries by practical men, *judices* (who were not lawyers), jurists (lawyers of renown), praetors (who were politicians) and, in the last centuries, emperors surrounded by highly qualified civil servants. Problems were dealt with as they turned up and were submitted to the jurists who gave their opinions and wrote books, or to the imperial government, which replied by rescript. The idea that the law was contained or even half hidden in some old book and had to be ascertained by the exegetical method was quite alien to the Roman world. Nor did Rome ever issue codes, as modern Europe did, although it did produce private or official collections of extant material. A look at the world history of law quickly shows that most civilisations have produced their law much as the Romans and the English did, by devising new ideas, techniques and rules or, if that was shunned, new fictions, to meet practical needs as they arose and as changing times required.[12] Only the European continent in the Middle Ages came to treat the law as a timeless revelation contained in a holy book: the *Corpus Juris* and the *Code Civil* became the lawyers' bibles. As legal perfection was embodied in them and as the *Corpus Juris* in particular was *ratio scripta*, 'reason put in writing', so legal science – and it was a bookish science rather than a practitioner's art – was based on great authoritative texts and could consist of nothing else than glosses and commentaries.[13]

Whether this was the best way of developing and studying law may be left an open question here, but on the scale of world history it certainly was an exceptional and remarkable way of doing things. Only Jewish and Muslim law seem comparable: for these other two 'peoples of the book'[14] the law was also a development of, and a gloss on, the one great law book of Revelation. But there are differences: Jewish and Muslim law contain religious commands, and their legal science was not severed from the original religious context, nor did it know the equivalent of the rational codes of the eighteenth and nineteenth centuries in Europe. The *Corpus Juris* and the science built upon it were legal and not religious and if Church law may have been regarded by some as part of theology, there was never any idea that the faculty of civil law could be considered part of that of divinity. There is another important difference in that both Jewish and Muslim law were based on divine command, whereas the *Corpus Juris* in the Middle Ages wielded no authority other than its own intrinsic quality. It had been issued as law by Justinian at a time when imperial authority had disappeared in the West, and his medieval successors never proclaimed the *Corpus* as law in their own territories, not to speak of the whole of western Europe. If it was supreme, it was not *ratione imperii*, but *imperio rationis*, i.e. not because of some imperial command, but at the behest of reason. It is amazing and probably unique that the medieval world suddenly accepted the great law book of a society that had been gone for centuries as its ultimate authority, and entirely reshaped its own law through scholastic glosses, disputations and commentaries on this venerable relic of a defunct world. Seen in this light, the English way of developing existing rules, modernising the courts and their procedure and gradually building up new case law or occasionally appealing to the lawgiver, but for the rest letting the professionals get on with their daily task of pleading and adjudicating, appears much the more normal. Thus it would seem that – if divergence or even deviation occurred – it was the continentals who diverged and the English who followed the common path.

4

WHICH IS BEST, CASE LAW, STATUTE LAW OR BOOK LAW?

So far the past, and the questions when and why common law and civil law originated, and when and why judges, legislators or scholars dominated the legal scene, have been discussed. It has not been asked which of these approaches was the best – in other words, the discussion has not gone beyond value-free propositions. Many historians believe that this is only as it should be: the historian's task is to describe and, if possible, to explain what happened, not to tell his reader what lessons he should draw from the past. There are, indeed, innumerable books and articles describing the organisation of governments and courts in a multitude of countries and periods, but although they enter into the most minute details, the reader may be sure he will not be told how good that particular government was for the people concerned. That is a philosophical question, a subjective political decision and that is taboo in scholarly historical work. Although it is not difficult to see many good reasons for this attitude, it is a legitimate desire on the part of the layman that the historian, who presumably knows the past best, should also try to answer some questions about the lessons to be drawn from mankind's experiences. It is well known that the Historical School has been reproached by leading jurists with being 'ultimately barren, because it could not consistently put any aim before men for which they should strive' and that 'in effect the historical method comes to the justification of what is, by simply asserting that it is'.[1]

What does history teach us about the advantages and disadvantages of the forms of government our ancestors have used or undergone? Since it seems to me that this is a reasonable question to ask a legal historian, I shall endeavour to say a few things about the specific value of legislation, case law and jurisprudence, as revealed by the study of the past.

Legislation has the advantage of binding certainty: the rules are laid down by a person or body in authority. If they are proclaimed in the form of a code, certainty is at its highest, for not only can the citizen know what the law is but, because of the comprehensive nature of the code, he has no reason to worry about all sorts of old and half forgotten (customary) rules that might suddenly appear from nowhere and spoil his legitimate expectations. The disadvantage of legislation is its lack of flexibility: the rules and the codes are laid down in precise texts, and stand until new legislation changes them. New legislation often lags behind the need of the times and new codes are very hard to establish; usually they are adapted, not replaced. The consequence is that the old cohesion is lost – for example, the *Code Civil* of 1804 is still valid in Belgium and France, although hundreds of articles have been dropped or replaced by mainly twentieth-century piecemeal legislation.

Case law is difficult to assess. Some say it has the advantage of certainty, because of *stare decisis*: if a court has adjudicated in a certain sense in one case, it will not change the law for someone else if a similar case comes along. It is true that this used to be a holy tenet of the common law and that the judges were so attached to this certainty that they were prepared to sacrifice justice and equity on its altar: it was better to observe an iniquitous or even absurd precedent for the sake of certainty, for if judges started to ignore precedents or throw them overboard, one of the pillars, possibly the main pillar of the common law, would be demolished.[2] It is in this light that one can understand the decision of the House of Lords in the late nineteenth century to consider itself bound by its own precedents. However, not all judges agree with this point of view; some claim that justice should prevail over certainty or, as one of them put it in the seventeenth century, a judge ought not to follow a bad precedent for 'that were to wrong every man having a like cause, because another was wronged before'.[3] It has been pointed out already that Lord Denning was a great champion of this view and that the House of Lords in 1966 changed its position and now feels free to reverse its own precedents.[4] It may be a gain for justice and flexibility that (some) courts are not bound by precedents which in our day and age are considered iniquitous, although they seemed perfectly equitable at the time they were first laid down, but it is a blow against certainty. In most cases, of course, *stare decisis* is still the rule, but one cannot be absolutely sure that the court will not reverse a precedent for some reason which it now considers imperative. It is bewildering to find one school of thought praising case law for its certainty, and another for its flexibility (this last point being particularly stressed by adversaries of codification). Nor are things made easier by certain judges believing, as has been pointed out before, that it is seldom difficult to get around a precedent when it seems to stand in the way of a desirable judgment. The following quotation from Lord Denning will give the reader something to ponder about: 'The truth is that the law is uncertain . . . no one can tell what the law is until the courts decide it. The judges do every day make law, though it is almost heresy to say so.'[5] One thing is in no doubt however: a weakness of case law is that it lacks a proper conceptual framework, and is very little given to generalisation.

Jurisprudence, on the other hand, comes into its own when the formulation of general principles is required: not only abstract concepts but also criticism and analysis of trends in legal thinking and in adjudication are its proper domain. There is no doubt that jurists can clarify and explain in a way that is neither the lawgiver's nor the judge's. The weakness of the schools is no less glaring. Their books – vast tomes *De citationibus*, for example – can be excruciatingly pedantic. Worse still, 'doctores certant': jurists love to disagree, to the great bewilderment of the courts and of their clients. Admittedly a *communis opinio* is sometimes established, but it is rare that not one dissenting voice can be unearthed from the tomes of the learned libraries. Unfortunately there was no medieval emperor to decide who was right, unlike the pope who could lay down the law in a decretal and decide by his apostolic authority whose learned opinion had won the day and was therefore to become law.

This brief and rather abstract description may not seem very helpful to some readers, who might prefer to tackle the problem from a more direct and personal point of view. Their reaction may be that whatever the merits of judge-made law in general, its quality to a very large extent will depend on the quality of the judges: one's appreciation of judge-made law (and judicial review of statutes) might depend on the personality and background of the judges. This is the human reality of the problem: judge-made law will be as good as the judges who made it (it can hardly be better). It would seem a good idea, therefore, to go somewhat deeper into the historical question as to the identity of the judges and who appointed them. A quick historical-comparative glance at this problem seems appropriate here.

THE JUDGES: AMATEURS AND PROFESSIONALS

In primitive times one assumes that justice was meted out without law courts: criminals were lynched, thieves who were caught red-handed were summarily hanged, family feuds served to settle disputes. But soon courts were organised, even though at first there seems to have been no compulsion to submit to them. The early judges acted more like arbiters, who have no authority unless disputes are freely put before them by the parties. A late reminder of this in a fully developed judicial system may be the freedom of accused criminals in medieval England to submit to the jury – 'to put themselves upon the land' – or not. Admittedly very hard pressure – literally speaking – was brought to bear on recalcitrants, but some preferred to be pressed to death in prison rather than submit to the jury's verdict of guilty which entailed not only loss of life, but the loss of all one's goods, i.e. the disinheritance of one's children and the end of the family fortunes.

The early courts were not composed of regular judges. Thus the Frankish *rachimburgii* were selected from the public for each given case and it was not until Charlemagne that the *scabini* (regular judges appointed for life) were instituted. They were in no way trained professionals, for their main occupation concerned military or agricultural matters, but a certain professionalism crept in, since they sat regularly, and normally for a good length of time. The late Middle Ages saw a slow growth of professionalism. In many towns the *scabini* or aldermen were appointed or elected for life, which gave them some judicial professionalism, but it should not be forgotten that they were politicians, administrators, businessmen and/or owners of urban land as well. Such concentration, and not separation of power was the rule: the same men made urban law, ran urban justice and led urban administration – many wielded economic power as well. In the royal courts real professional judges made their appearance and as judicial professionalism grew, the participation of the public diminished.

In Homer's *Iliad* there is a story of a case in an early Greek court. It occurs in the description of one of the scenes on Achilles' famous shield, beautifully decorated by Hephaistus, the divine blacksmith. A crowd was depicted in the market place, where a dispute was going on about a *wergeld*, i.e. the blood-price of a man. The judges to whom the parties were willing to appeal sat in a sacred circle on polished stones. Each one of them took the herald's staff as he rose to propose a judgment. Before them lay two nuggets of gold, destined for the elder who gave the fairest proposal according to the acclaim of the people.[6] A few points deserve to be highlighted here. The people participated directly, as they did in Germanic Antiquity, showing their approval by the clatter of their arms. They did not, however, propose judgments (let alone pronounce them). That was for the judges, venerable old men, who did not deliberate together or reach a consensus, but proposed judgments under the cheers of the crowd, which gave the best judge a reward. The court sat surrounded by formal, even sacred elements: the circle, the polished stones, the herald's staff. This scene, *mutatis mutandis*, could have taken place in the early Middle Ages, where active participation of the public and non-professional judges, acting under the impact of the crowd, was well known. In the course of the centuries all this was changed. The crowd was eliminated in various degrees and at various stages. Far from awarding a prize for the best judgment proposal, the crowd was threatened with heavy fines for contradicting the pronouncements of the urban courts: the judges themselves decided which was the best judgment. In modern times the public was often discarded altogether, as business was conducted *in camera*. Where the people continued to be admitted, they were under a constant threat of being fined for contempt of court if they ventured to express their views too noisily or impolitely.

As the role of the public diminished, so the role of the professional judge increased. The phases of the progress are well known. At the starting point, in the 'first Middle Ages', i.e. roughly up until the twelfth century, there was hardly any professionalism in the sense of judges receiving specific training and making adjudication their main activity. There was only a certain measure insofar as certain judges, by sitting on law cases for many years, acquired a practical knowledge of the law and the forms of process. Some of these early judges were feudal lords holding a curia with their vassals or Carolingian *scabini* sitting in the court of the *comes* of the *pagus* (or their descendants in various parts of the Carolingian Empire), but others were peasants in manorial courts, sheriffs in county courts or burgesses and bailiffs in borough courts. None of these people had been formally trained or had adjudication as his main occupation. Compare this with the present-day situation where the courts have become thoroughly professional, to the point that on the Continent even the magistrates at the lowest level are required to be university graduates in law. Such professionalism, however widespread, is not complete. In England the magistrates (the justices of the peace) are not engaged full-time (nor are they salaried) and are not university graduates in law (and often not university graduates at all) – and it should not be forgotten that almost all minor misdemeanours pass through the magistrates' hands. This situation is not a modern freak, but belongs to

England's oldest traditions. It can be described as the dichotomy between a very small number of highly professional, highly trained and highly paid judges at the top, almost all in London (High Court, Court of Appeal, Law Lords and stipendiary magistrates), and a vast number of non-professional and untrained J.P.'s, now magistrates, at the lower echelons throughout the country.[7] If one remembers that for centuries even the cases before senior judges were decided by juries as far as the question of fact was concerned, one understands the importance of the untrained and unlearned element in dispensing justice in England, and incidentally how cheap it all was for the crown: juries and J.P.'s drew no salaries! On the Continent professionalism is more widespread, since even the lower courts throughout the provinces are manned by graduates and professionals, who are numbered in their thousands instead of their hundreds. This is an old contrast with England, for whereas the three common-law courts could manage with twelve judges, the Parlement of Paris counted fifty-one by 1297 and by the eighteenth century as many as 240. In the meantime twelve new Parlements had been created and the total membership of these thirteen appellate courts had risen to over 1,200.[8] Around 1900 there were in France some 5,000 to 6,000 judges, in England (High Court, Court of Appeal and Lords) forty (the judicial establishment of England in 1727 consisted of seventeen judges; by 1875, when the population had increased more than five-fold, the number of judges was only twenty-seven).[9] Plans in 1933 to add another five led to protest because a lowering of the quality was feared – nowadays the number has risen to approximately one hundred (there are also approximately 280 lower judges in the County Courts). Nevertheless, even on the Continent professionalism is not absolute: military, commercial and labour tribunals contain some non-lawyers among their adjudicating personnel.

The main stages of this historic phenomenon on the Continent can be outlined as follows. The earliest professionalisation took place within the Church. Until *c.* 1200 the old *curia episcopalis* used to deal with legal and much other business. It was more like a people's court, for it consisted not only of various clerics from the bishop's entourage but also of older, leading laymen. It discussed and adjudicated in a traditional way and without being bound to strict procedures and rules. Before the twelfth century was out, this rather amateurish way of doing justice began to give way to the bishop's official and his court. Here adjudication lay firmly in the hands of a trained lawyer, a university graduate, who applied the strict rules of the brand-new Roman-canonical procedure described in the *ordines judiciarii*, the first fruits of the science of procedure. There is some uncertainty whether the official was the product of this new procedure or the other way around. Did the introduction of the new learned judge lead to that of the new learned procedure, or did the introduction of the latter necessitate the rise of the former? This is a difficult and possibly otiose question since both phenomena were roughly contemporary. Whatever the causal nexus, the thirteenth century saw the establishment of the bishop's official's court as the ordinary local tribunal in the western Church and this was without any doubt the breakthrough on the road to professional judges everywhere. The professional local judge in lay courts, however, was still a long way away. The legists took their seats first in the great central courts of the kingdoms. There too a coincidence between a change in personnel and in procedure can be noticed: round the middle of the thirteenth century King Louis IX established his Parlement at Paris and introduced the learned procedure into his kingdom, to replace the old ordeals and combat. Other countries followed this lead. In the Low Countries legists appeared in the service of the counts of Flanders in the late thirteenth century, and when Duke Charles the Bold installed his Parlement at Malines in 1473, it was so full of them that the revolt on his death in 1477 demanded and obtained its abolition. On the whole the great central courts were popular with litigants, who flocked to them: even in times of international tension litigants from the county of Flanders went on appeal to the Parlement of Paris.[10] Cynics will say that this proves nothing else than the endless drive of litigants to carry on fighting their cases until even the remotest possibility of success is exhausted. I believe, however, that the popularity of these central courts, which was already noticeable in England under King Henry II, was to a large extent based on the expectation that better justice could be had there, because the procedure was more rational and accurate and because the judges were better trained; they were also more remote than the local judicial assemblies and could therefore be expected to be more neutral. The juries, of course, were panels of local people, whose neutrality might be doubtful, although clearly they were deemed more reliable than ordeals and judicial combat. The parties apparently – and understandably – had greater trust in the professional judges: the success of the Parlement of Paris was so great that provincial Parlements had to be created, and as has already been seen, the papal curia was so overburdened in the twelfth century that papal judges delegate were appointed to lighten the work in Rome.

Whereas professionalisation made solid progress in the central courts, the urban judicial institutions were slow to follow suit. Thus the aldermen (*schepenen*, *échevins*) of the

large Flemish towns who dealt with numerous and important cases (they had full jurisdiction in first instance in
criminal and civil cases), were extremely slow to welcome
university graduates among their ranks. Before the sixteenth century it is very rare indeed to find a graduate on an
urban bench and if the urban judges needed advice on
questions involving Roman or canon law, they asked their
pensionaries, who were employed by the towns for that
purpose. Only in modern times have the pressure of Roman
law and the enormous expansion of law studies of the
sixteenth century led to a real strengthening of the graduate
element on the urban benches. This same century saw an
extraordinary explosion in the numbers of law students all
over Europe, in the English Inns of Court as well as in the
continental universities. The armies of new graduates did
not all enter the Profession, since the law was considered a
suitable preparation for gracious and urban living and a
law degree was a desirable status symbol (in the eighteenth
century this fashion was on the wane, together with the
numbers of law students). Nevertheless, many new graduates did find employment in government and the courts.[11]
Nor was the process of professionalism a mere success-
story: there was a good deal of resistance against the rise of
the graduates and their way of doing justice. This was
particularly the case in German lands, where bitter complaints were heard during the Peasants' Wars about the
slow and costly procedure and endless procrastination of
the learned law and its courts. In Switzerland, of course, the
famous cry 'we do not want to hear of Bartolus and Baldus'
was uttered, as a protest against Roman law and its
servants on the bench.[12] Much later the government could
still get into serious trouble when it tried to impose
rationalisation and professionalisation. This was demonstrated in the Austrian Netherlands, for when the Emperor

Joseph II decided to streamline judicial organisation and to carry out a drastic programme of professionalisation, so many holders of small local courts felt hurt in their pride and their pocket that their discontent was one of the factors in the outbreak of a full-scale, albeit short-lived revolution.

The rise in professionalism went hand in hand with a rise in the status of the judges. They achieved their independence: the Stuarts still regarded 'their' judges as their servants and on a famous occasion Sir Edward Coke was dismissed, but from the early eighteenth century onwards they were no longer anyone's servants and the king could only dismiss them if both Houses of Parliament requested it: they were, in fact, irremovable. It should be realised, however, that this principle, which stands today, is applicable only to senior judges: the mass of magistrates can be dismissed by the chancellor, if he thinks they ought not to remain on the bench. On the Continent things were somewhat different. Frederick the Great in Prussia did not hesitate to reprimand and punish judges who, according to him, had failed in their duty nor to use his *Machtspruch* against their *Rechtspruch*. Thus in a famous case of 1779, the judges who had given judgment against miller Arnold were arrested and subjected to criminal prosecution. In January 1780 five judges were sent to jail for a year and dismissed.[13] Much more dramatic, and even tragic, had been the case of young Hans Hermann von Katte. This lieutenant in a Berlin regiment had helped crown prince Frederick (the future Frederick the Great) in an abortive plan to escape from the authority of his father, King Frederick William I of Prussia. He was arrested and court-martialled and as the judges were evenly divided whether to impose life imprisonment or the death sentence, the court pronounced the former. The king demanded the death sentence and sent the case back to the same court, which maintained its position. As supreme judge of the nation, he thereupon pronounced the death sentence himself, and von Katte was executed on 6 November 1730, aged twenty-six.

Those were the days of the concentration of power, the king being head of the executive, the legislature and the judiciary. In France the immovability of the judges was largely achieved by the sale of offices: a purchased seat in a Parlement was private property and nobody could take it away, for this would have been theft. But even in the eighteenth century there were still two notions that gave the king of France ultimate control over his judges. The king always had a reserved jurisdiction, i.e. he could bring before his own Council cases which interested him and impose his own sentence, even after the Parlement of Paris had pronounced judgment (which normally was the last word on the case). He might not be able to deprive the judges of their offices, but he could punish them for obstruction and send them into internal banishment, as Chancellor Maupeou did with the members of the recalcitrant Parlement of Paris, which was ever intent on thwarting royal reforms. On the night of 19 January 1771 musketeers delivered to each one of them a *lettre de cachet* ordering him to state whether he was or not prepared to return to his duties: this followed a bout of particular obstreperousness, when the Parlement had defied a *lit de justice* (the most solemn royal form of command) and even gone on strike. Nearly all refused to give this assurance and 130 of them were at once exiled to remote and wild places such as the Auvergne and deprived of their offices.[14] This was an extreme step and the royal government soon backtracked: the irremovability of the judges was on the whole respected as long as the ancient regime lasted.

It is interesting to observe what happened afterwards in France, at a time when the security of office for the senior judges was never in dispute in Britain. The appointment of irremovable judges was one of the earliest aspects of the old order to be thrown out. In accordance with attacks in the National Assembly on the *aristocratie thémistique*, 'the most dangerous of all aristocracies',[15] it was decided, on 5 May 1790, nine months after the sale of offices was abolished, to introduce an elective judiciary, enjoying temporary office. After much soul searching the term was fixed at six years. Not long afterwards, Napoleon, who had 'ended the revolution', reintroduced appointive judges: the justices of the peace were elected until the Year X of the Revolution and after that date the election of judges disappeared from French public law, except for two short episodes.[16]

The normal situation in the course of the nineteenth century therefore was judicial appointment, and, on principle, ever since the Constitution of the year VIII, so was the irremovability of the judges. In fact, however, political passion from time to time gained the upper hand and 'epurations' were carried out to eliminate judges for party political reasons. Recent research has thrown some precious new light on these shocking events. In spite of certain solemn declarations the Restoration following Napoleon's fall did not respect the irremovability of the judiciary, since it was understood that only royal appointment guaranteed tenure. Hence between 1815 and 1818 almost 300 judges were eliminated from the royal courts, including several court and chamber presidents. The revolution of 1830, under the 'July Monarchy', led to a vast 'epuration'. The republic of February 1848 expressly abolished the irremovability as being incompatible with a republican regime and suspended judges who were reputed to be irremovable. In 1852 the return to a Napoleonic regime led to the institution of the *Commissions Mixtes* which prosecuted and punished numerous republican sympathisers, including a number of judges who were dismissed and sent into exile: some of them had been guilty of not being present at a *Te Deum* in honour of Napoleon III. In 1870 the republicans, of course, took their revenge: some of the dismissed judges of 1852 returned to the Palace of Justice and some of their erstwhile enemies were in their turn dismissed. A law of 30 August 1883, under the Third Republic, suspended the irremovability of the judges for three months and 614 of them were dismissed for being hostile to the republican regime (royalism was then still a live force in the country). This hostility could have been shown by not greeting the prefect of the department or by going to church. The law of 1883 only remained on the statute book for six months.[17]

The requirements for obtaining higher functions in the judiciary were largely the same in England as in France. The main question was that of status, i.e. of belonging to the aristocracy or the gentry. In England landed wealth could be somewhat more important than money, but the latter was obviously crucial in France where offices were for sale to the nobility. In England the status requirement could consist of the heavy cost of staying at one of the Inns of Court (and in the nineteenth century the cost of the public schools and studies in Oxford and Cambridge) or in outright laws reserving places in the Inns to members of the aristocracy or gentry.[18] Even the justices of the peace had to fulfil a stiff wealth requirement. To be rich was still very important in France in the nineteenth century. The land-owning class was well represented in the courts and people were unashamed about the money factor: letters have survived from candidates who wrote to the minister saying that they were eminently suitable to become judges because they lived in the finest house in town and this clearly demonstrated their financial standing and stability.[19] It is true that in France the formal intellectual requirement was somewhat different from England, since a university degree in law was necessary. However, one should see this in its true perspective: the demands upon the students were light, examinations not taken too seriously, and there were universities that sold diplomas.

Rising independence equalled rising power. The judges in course of time were elevated above their fellow citizens. It is a transition that might be described as 'from judgment by peers to judgment by superiors'. The latter situation had prevailed in the late Roman Empire, where judgment lay in the hands of imperial appointees, and was dominant in the Church, at least since the creation of the bishops' officials: laymen appeared in Church courts to be judged by bishops' deputies and in last instance by the clergy of the papal court. The hierarchical idea was very pronounced, for as Gratian put it 'there are two sorts of Christians, the clergy and the laity' and it was clear that the latter was subjected to the former.[20] The feudal world, on the other hand, had a very different approach. It felt very strongly that people should be judged by their equals, by men belonging to their own natural milieu, their own social group, and not by their superiors, nor of course by their inferiors. A superior might hold the court in which his people appeared, but judgment was found by the latter's equals. Thus, to quote the archetypal situation, vassals should be judged in their lord's court by their co-vassals. This, incidentally, was one of the considerations against appeal, for appearing in a higher court normally meant appearing before superiors instead of equals. This feudal idea was prevalent in other sections of medieval society: peasants appeared in the manor court, burgesses appeared in the borough court. One of the most famous expressions of this principle occurs in that very feudal document, the Magna Carta of 1215. Art. 38, which lays down the great principles of the rule of law and due process, stipulates that various sanctions against persons and goods can only be imposed 'by a just judgment of one's peers or according to the law of the land'. The same idea existed forcefully around the same time in towns which had organised a commune, where elected and sworn leaders (*jurati electi*) were the judges in communal conflicts.

The idea was to some extent lost in the course of the following centuries. It was half lost in towns where appointed or co-opted *scabini* were the judges of their fellow citizens, for they had been elevated to a higher position by the ruler, who also forbade criticism of their judgments. The idea was completely lost when the great central courts of the late medieval monarchies were established. There the judges were royal appointees, sometimes sitting with the king himself, who judged his subjects without any regard to equality of rank; quite often the legists in the Parlement of Paris would be of bourgeois extraction and yet sit in judgment over noblemen and land-owning bishops. In the eyes of the law, as they administered it, there were no superior classes, inferior groups or equals: everyone was a subject of the king and when he appeared in the king's court he received justice from the hands of the king's judges. This led to ill-feeling amongst the peers of France, who objected to appearing in the Parlement of Paris before some of the gentry or even smaller fry, and demanded in vain to be judged by their peers and nobody else. A famous example was presented by the count of Flanders' refusal to submit to the Parlement of Paris in the days of King Philip IV the Fair. The trend was forcefully continued in modern times, but even today some traces of the old idea of judgment by peers can be found in the jurisdiction of military courts over soldiers and mercantile courts over merchants.

Another illustration of the increasing power of judges can be found in the evolution of the law of evidence. Initially judges watched passively the result of the ordeal: it was for the parties or their champions to do their best and for the judges to take note of the result and to see the sign God had given to the court and the public. The knowledge or the feeling of the judges was irrelevant, for if the plaintiff slew the defendant in judicial combat that settled the plea, whatever the judges might think about the merits of the case. Nowadays, the other extreme has been reached and everything is put on the shoulders of the judge or the jury, and it is their conviction, attained after careful weighing of all the evidence, that decides the case. In this regime all depends on the *conviction intime* of the judge or the jury. The Continent has passed through a curious intermediate stage, where the judge certainly was expected actively to weigh the evidence and to strive for the truth of the matter, but was not given complete liberty as to how to reach his judgment. It was the stage of the *preuves savantes*, the system of evidence of the learned procedure. The schools had worked out mathematical formulas for the proof-value of various elements of evidence: confession, witnesses *de visu et auditu*, circumstantial evidence, etc. And only if proof was fully established according to this arithmetic was the judge entitled to pronounce a verdict of guilty: his freedom to reach a conscientious conviction was hampered by legal rules. Thus, to give a simple example, if there was one witness *de visu et auditu*, that would be half proof; if there was also an indication (e.g. the man accused of robbery suddenly started spending a great deal of money) that would be another quarter proof, and confession under torture might yield the missing quarter and make up a full proof (*plena probatio*) against the accused. The *preuves légales* belong to the past now, but the strict rules of evidence in English law sometimes remind us of them, as they were also formed to discipline the freedom of juries and judges in reaching verdicts. It has been argued recently that it was the admission of the judge's *conviction intime* as sufficient for condemnation which made torture (and obtaining confessions) superfluous in the later eighteenth century, and that this shift in legal doctrine was responsible for the disappearance of torture rather than the well known agitation of the philosophical authors of that period.[21]

THE COURTS AND THEIR CREATORS

That the law is as good as the judges make it is a truism. It may be less strikingly so on the Continent than in England, the land of judge-made law *par excellence*, but it is still a statement of general validity. It therefore seems pertinent to ask the historical question who made the judges who made the law. The problem has not been subjected yet to comprehensive research and it will suffice here to give some preliminary remarks, in the hope that they may be followed up by more detailed enquiries. At first sight the main divide seems to be between appointive and elective judges – appointed by the government or elected by the people.[22] But there is a third category, those who became judges by co-optation.

Since nomination by the ruler and election by the people are a strong reminder of W. Ullmann's famous dichotomy of the descending and ascending theory of power, his model will be used as a tool to distinguish
Type I, the descending theory, for appointment by the ruler
Type II, the ascending theory, for election by the people.[23]
In trying to attribute the historical methods of selection of judges to one of these two types, it quickly becomes apparent that a third is needed: that of a caste of aristocra-

tic judges who are neither nominated (except formally) nor elected, but hold their positions by heredity or co-optation. The heredity can either be by blood, as in the old House of Lords where all the lords effectively sat in judgment, or by inheritance of the seats bought by an ancestor. That this oligarchy of judges cannot be given a proper place in Ullmann's system is one indication among others that his scheme needs to be emended, because it leaves out what might be called the 'regime of the notables' (whom Max Weber called the *honoratiores* and the Greeks the oligarchs). This regime came into its own after the fall of the old-style monarchy and before modern democracy took over. A classic example is the Belgian constitution of 1831, which vested supreme power in a parliament elected by 1% of the population. Clearly, this was not an example of the descending theory of power, for although there was a king, effective political power lay in the hands of an elected parliament, and a government supported by a majority in that parliament. But it was not an example of the ascending theory either for, although parliament was chosen, the electorate was so restricted that nobody could seriously pretend that its power came from the people: it was that of a small upper group of wealthy citizens. Hence there is a need for a Type III in the analysis, that of power in the hands of an aristocracy of blood or money. In the present day and age the nearest thing to Type III is probably the power of the communist party, which forms a co-opted elite of about 5% of the population, or less, and has the constitutional task of leading every aspect of public life, since it represents the politically conscious section of the nation.

So we shall use as an analytic tool a Type I: appointment by the highest political power, a Type II: election by the people, and a Type III: a caste of judges based on descent from the nobility or the gentry or purchase of office and, generally speaking, fulfilling property requirements.

In historic Europe Type I was on principle predominant, insofar as most judges were appointed by the monarch, although in reality that freedom of appointment was nibbled away by the sale of offices or exclusive appointment from a very limited milieu. Thus the French king in modern times appointed his judges, but the sale of the offices to the highest bidder severely curtailed his freedom. Thus also from the Middle Ages onwards the English kings, who appointed the higher judges, had to take them from the ranks of the serjeants at law, i.e. senior barristers attached to the royal courts: the serjeants had the monopoly of pleading in the Court of Common Pleas and of judicial appointments in the two benches. In course of time the servants became masters. It is clear that initially the kings freely appointed judges in the new royal courts, but control of these nominations was eroded in various ways so that in fact an imperceptible transition to Type III took place.

Type II was predominant with Germanic peoples and in the early Middle Ages, when the assemblies of freemen selected eminent persons to sit at each meeting of the *mallus* or *thing*; in the reign of Charlemagne they were replaced by *scabini*, royal appointees for life. In the autonomous communes of the eleventh and twelfth centuries the judicial function, as has been said before, was in the hands of *jurati electi*, sworn judges and officials of the urban commune, elected by its members. The Italian *podestà* was also chosen by the commune and the efforts of Frederick II to impose his own nominees was one of the bones of contention between him and the Italian towns. What he thought of elected judges and officials can be gathered from articles I, 50 and I,10,7 of his *Liber Augustalis*, which stipulate that towns which create *podestà*s, consuls or other officials by authority of some custom or by election of the people shall 'suffer perpetual desolation and that all the men of that city should be held as perpetual forced labourers ... and anyone who has received any of the aforesaid offices should be punished by death'.[24] It has already been seen that modern France introduced an elective judiciary on several occasions – in 1790, 1848 and 1882 – but always for very brief periods.

Type III became all the more conspicuous: it was constantly encroaching on Type I. Urban aldermen in Flanders, for example, were initially appointed by the count, but already in the twelfth century the pressure towards co-optation was mounting. Thus the famous borough charter granted to the main Flemish towns by Count Philip of Alsace (1157–91) stipulated firmly in its art. 24 that these judges were to be appointed according to the will of the count 'and not otherwise'.[25] In the thirteenth century the rising tide of co-optation could not be stemmed any more, and for the rest of the Middle Ages a great variety of systems was worked out to give the count of Flanders some say in the appointment of the new urban magistrates, but leaving a good deal to co-optation, which suited the urban 'patriciate' well. The problem has been carefully studied, but is much too complex to be summarised here.[26] In the feudal world Type III was clearly predominant. Ever since the second half of the ninth century the heredity of fiefs made headway and since vassals were also judges sitting in their lords' courts, this meant that judicial functions in feudal courts were or became hereditary. In modern times simple and straightforward co-optation, as a means of self-perpetuation of an influential group was rare (as the practice still is today with the election of new Benchers of the Inns of Court by the sitting Benchers). All the more frequent were other ways of restricting the monarch's liberty of appointment. This was achieved in the Middle Ages, when the new councillors in the Parlement of Paris were appointed by the king from a list of three names put forward by that court. The first signs of the Parlement's control over the entry of new members occurred in the 1340s; shortly after 1400 co-optation by the Parlement of its new members was expressly authorised, but this was later replaced by a royal appointment from a panel of three candidates presented by the Parlement.[27] In modern times the sale of offices in France strongly limited, as has been said before, the royal freedom of appointment, as did the fact that, in Germany, various courts had by law to be occupied by members of the nobility. The English king's freedom, as has been seen, was severely restricted by the monopoly of the serjeants at law, an aristocracy of barristers who were selected for their ability, of course, but also by birth and fortune. The House of Lords, which became the highest court in the land, was composed of members of the hereditary peerage (and a few bishops) and they could all sit in judgment on cases of appeal – a practice that was only dropped around the middle of the nineteenth century in favour of a limited number of professional lawyers taken from their ranks. This step, incidentally, was a good illustration of a certain English way of doing things, for the lay Lords (i.e. those Lords who were not Law Lords) lost their legal right to vote on appeals not through some enactment or authoritative pronouncement, but because after 1844 such votes were never given again (which shows the strength of convention); when some years later a lay Lord who felt very strongly about a certain case tried to intervene, he was simply ignored.[28]

The overall impression of this brief survey is that in Old Europe, formally speaking, the appointment by the sovereign predominated, but that in reality the judicial caste and the legal profession were very much in control.

It seems worthwhile to conclude these paragraphs with a look at the present-day situation in Europe and the United States: it will quickly appear that mixtures of the three Types are the rule, but that the dosage of the ingredients varies markedly from country to country. Discussion will be limited to three examples, one from the continent of Europe, one from the British Isles and one from America.

Belgium offers an interesting example of a mixture of the three types. Type I is represented insofar as formally the appointment of all judges is made by royal decree (also, the royal pardon may formally be seen as a relic of royal judicial power). Type II is indirectly represented insofar as various elected political bodies (provincial councils and the Senate) play a role in the proposition of names for appointment (the jury in criminal cases can also be seen as a popular element in this connection). Type III is represented because various courts also propose lists of names for appointment by the king.[29] There are no longer any financial but only intellectual requirements, i.e. a law degree, which is deemed sufficient: there are no examinations for entering the judiciary (or the bar) and there are no special schools for the training of prospective judges.

In England Type I is represented by the appointment by the crown, i.e. by the Prime Minister or the Lord Chancellor (who is a member of the government), who can exert a certain discretion in choosing between the candidates.[30] Type II is only very indirectly present because the government's power is based on a majority in the elected chamber, and the jury is also a popular element. Type III is present in greater strength, because the higher judges are chosen from the very small number of Queen's Counsels, i.e. that top group of successful and experienced barristers who have 'taken silk'. They are themselves selected by the legal profession. The Law Lords, the highest judicial authority in the land, are normally selected from the ranks of the other higher judges, i.e. the High Court and the Court of Appeal. There is no strict requirement for a university degree (in law or something else). There are no examinations for the judiciary, but there are examinations for the bar; there is no special school for judges. The overall impression is that both in Belgium and England Type I is weak and that for the rest Type II is somewhat stronger in Belgium and Type III somewhat stronger in England.

In the United States Type I is found in the appointment of all federal judges and particularly of the judges in the United States Supreme Court, who are appointed by the President, but not without the intervention of the Senate. In many states the governor appoints the judiciary. Type II is represented indirectly in that the President and the governors are elected by the people and that the Senate, an elected body, has a role to play; it is strong, of course, in those states where the judges are elected by the people. Type III is very weak: one can mention only the fact that the American Bar Association informally submits a list to the President of the United States, who may be said to consult the Profession, and that a similar action is taken by the state Bar Associations in connection with the appointments of governors. Finally the jury, most active in both civil and criminal cases, adds another strong element to Type II, all the more so since after the Revolution the role of the judges was restricted, with instructions to the jury, for example, which are usual in England, being forbidden.[31]

The conclusion to be drawn from all these observations is obvious: the democratic – Type II – element in the United States' judicial system is remarkably pronounced, Type I is not without importance, but Type III, the oligarchic element so typical for the European tradition, is almost non-existent.

Which of these three types is the best is hard to deduce from the lessons of history. Moreover, the question has some connection with that posed some time ago, about the respective qualities of judges', politicians' and scholars' law. Indeed the law made by politicians in legislative assemblies is clearly close to Type II, whereas the law made by the European type of judiciary is historically linked to Type III, and the law made by a king-legislator is clearly linked to Type I. It is proposed, therefore, to take up again the question of the respective merits of the three sources of the law. They clearly reflect different values and visions of society and are often in conflict with each other.

CODIFICATION: A WEAPON AGAINST THE JUDICIARY

Codification was historically a weapon against the judiciary, or the caste of the *noblesse de robe* who owned their offices and invoked nebulous general principles that were nowhere written down. It served also against the doctors of law who bandied about learned quotations from books that were a thousand years old or from other doctors who buried justice under heavy tomes, full of contradictions and fit only to lead the common man astray. Complaints about Roman law in the enlightened eighteenth century are eloquent witnesses to this criticism. In contrast to all this, legislation by elected representatives, issued in the form of codes, was the dearest wish of the people. The legislation of the French Revolution was the most eloquent expression of this sentiment. It was aimed against privilege and discrimination, for freedom from personal subjection and legal equality and even, in some phases of the Revolution, for economic equality, the abundant production of material goods and the sharing of wealth. Legislation stood for popular law, for innovation; Roman law and Parlements stood for immobility and the *ancien régime*.

It is not necessary to belabour this well known aspect of the French Revolution, but it is less generally appreciated that the English revolutionaries of the seventeenth century, the Puritans, were equally enthusiastic about legislation and that their policies form an interesting illustration of the old contrast between – in F. A. Hayek's terminology – *nomos*, the law made by the judges and *thesis*, the law edited by the legislator.[32] As Roscoe Pound wrote, 'the Commonwealth in England brought forth a great outburst of legislative activity' and 'one of the first fruits of Massachusetts was an attempt to set the statute book in order and its preface contains a defense of legislative lawmaking'.[33] Indeed, the Laws and Liberties of Massachusetts of 1648 are an interesting document for students of codification, and may well be considered the first modern code of the western world. The document was the fruit of more than ten years' preparatory work and was comprehensive, as it contained not only a complete declaration of the laws, privileges, rights and duties that prevailed in the colony, but also extended to criminal, property and family law as well. It remained fundamental in Massachusetts throughout the colonial period and was imitated by other colonies in New England. It was more than a simple compilation of existing norms and constituted a new and conscious effort to establish norms appropriate to the new circumstances of life in America. It therefore did not hesitate to change or abandon English common law elements, notably in the field of procedure. Its origin, of course, was to be found in the desire to obtain legal certainty and to combat judicial discretion, but since this Puritan colony was biblically inspired the veneration for the written word was a strong contributing factor.[34] As far as England was concerned, it was, as has been seen, through legislation and even codification that the Puritan government hoped to reform English law, paying no heed to the warning that 'Our laws are sacred, pious, good, merciful and just ... and he must forfeit the whole reason of man who desires a change'.[35]

As against all this conscious and sometimes radical innovation, judge-made law normally reflects the views of the members of the establishment who man the courts. The judiciary, so often an expression of the ruling oligarchy, prizes social and economic stability above all else and exudes the conservatism inherent in the awe for old precedents and the aversion to setting new ones. This oligarchy respects property and accepts inequality and privilege: these eminent *oligoi* are best placed to control the law – if not to make it – and to keep society on an even keel. This is the judge-made law that resisted so well in England and France, until its profound fall in the latter, when the Revolution 'chained' the judges to prevent further harm. The question may well be asked why the continental judge, particularly in France, was so ignominiously dethroned, while his English colleague continued to occupy a very high if not exalted position. Here are a few observations which, of course, are far from exhaustive. England had her revolution some hundred and fifty years before France and its long term result was a strengthening of the judge-made common law. The English revolution had also taken place in a mental climate that still equated good law with old law, whereas the eighteenth-century faith in progress produced a belief that old law meant bad law and that only new law was good law – hence the radical change resulting from the French, as compared to the English, Revolution. Moreover the extreme element in the English revolution was more thoroughly wiped out by the Restoration than happened in

France after the various regimes of 1792–1815: Louis XVIII did not abrogate the Napoleonic codes.

LAW PROFESSORS SERVE THE POWERS THAT BE

And what does professors' law reflect? In contrast with the judge and the lawgiver the jurist has no direct power, cannot send anyone to prison, or proclaim laws. The best he can do is to try and influence those in power, or simply serve them. The latter seems to be the main historic role of the jurists. When Frederick Barbarossa was playing the great Roman emperor, four leading glossators were ready to define his powers in wide and truly imperial terms. This obviously pleased the emperor, but infuriated some of their colleagues, who felt that they betrayed the cause of the Italian communes. Thus Placentinus, a younger contemporary who taught Roman law in Mantua, Bologna and Montpellier, accused them of having behaved 'impiously, most falsely and against their own consciences'.[36] When, in the following century, the Italian communes seemed successfully to have resisted the monarchy, the doctors of Bologna entered into their service, to the disgust of Frederick II who, as has been seen, founded his own university at Naples with doctors who saw the *Corpus Juris* through his eyes and would properly educate his judges and his functionaries.

Things were little different in England in the seventeenth century, when some lawyers (Coke, Selden and Noy) were on Parliament's side and the crown could count on others (Ellesmere, Bacon, Heath), which caused one historian to remark that 'one of the principal characteristics of lawyers is that they are always found on both sides of any legal question'.[37]

As jurists are easily prepared to serve the powers that be,

so autocrats like to make use of them. Napoleon used four jurists to write his *Code Civil* (others had served to write the codes of the *droit intermédiaire*) and promptly forbade the lawyers to write commentaries on it: he did not want learned theories obscuring the clarity of his beloved law book, comprehensive and accessible to all. German and Austrian autocrats had not behaved differently, using diligent jurists-civil servants, and then forbidding the consultation of anyone but the lawgiver in case of doubt. The jurists of the Exegetical School served the bourgeois nineteenth century and its codes very well, and others began to criticise them when the great social movement of the end of the century launched new men on a bid for power. Savigny had spoken for Prussian conservatism when he attacked legislation and above all codification and claimed that the jurists were best placed to know the historic law of the people. He distrusted the arrogance and pride of the legislator and rejected the idea of chance and arbitrary origins of the law: law could not be made as the instrument of some deliberate policy, it arose from the innermost life of the nation.[38] Jurists, although sometimes indispensable, are not really popular with autocrats, because one never knows what conclusions they may draw in their pedantic, obscure and over-subtle volumes. They are not popular with the general public either, because they talk above people's heads and make simple things complicated. 'Englishmen do not love lawyers' said F. W. Maitland, 'and the law they have loved they did not think of as lawyers' law.'[39] Small wonder that the French Revolution abolished the law faculties by statute in 1793 and that in the new public schools elementary lessons in law were put on the curriculum to 'create virtuous citizens'[40] – these were the citizens who would not really engage in litigation, so it was hoped, because the *préliminaire de conciliation* would make that superfluous. In England learned jurists were ignored by the bench, so that far from influencing the course of the law, they were not even allowed to serve those who commanded it.

The jurists' only chance of having real influence on the future was to try and convince either the autocrats, the oligarchs or the revolutionary masses, who, they hoped, would one day issue codes that might incorporate their ideas. The followers of the 'law of reason' in the eighteenth century, who influenced the codes of the enlightened monarchs and of the French Revolution and Jeremy Bentham, who deeply influenced the liberal parliaments of the nineteenth century and their modernisation of the law, exemplify this. The great popes of the classical canon law were the one exception, as has been seen: they were at the same time jurists and supreme lawgivers, free to impose their doctrine through their own legislation.

That jurists have often been servants and instruments of the powers that be, is undeniable. This does not mean that one should forget about the others who have followed their own conscience and intellectual insight independently of, or even against, the rulers of the world, and legal science is much indebted to them.

EIGHT CRITERIA OF GOOD LAW

But let us return to our question as to which is the better law, that of the judge, the legislator or the scholar. It seems to me that we must first ask ourselves what constitutes good law. Is it possible to find criteria which command a wide consensus? The diversity of opinions in this day and age is so great that one sometimes despairs that there are any propositions on which general agreement is possible. For example, one might imagine that absolute respect for human life is such a proposition, until one remembers the controversy around the death penalty and abortion and realises how even that seemingly obvious norm is controversial. Or take another generalisation, that intellectual freedom is preferable to unfreedom. This at first sight obvious notion looks more doubtful when one realises that intellectual freedom is unknown in large parts of the world in regimes that seem quite acceptable to the inhabitants, so that one wonders whether intellectual discipline imposed from above does not suit many people better than the liberty – and the duty – of forming their own critical judgment. One can nevertheless make an attempt to define some criteria for a good legal system.

Incorruptible and impartial judges. That this is a universal ideal is at first sight irrefutable. There are nevertheless problems as soon as one looks further than gross corruption for large sums of money or partiality for reasons of kinship or political allegiance. There are more subtle forms of corruption, such as the material and psychological advantages heaped upon judges by the established regime so as to bind them to it. And it may be doubted whether judges, being human and having their own values and views on society, can ever be as impartial as a computer, which has no heart. Also, certain regimes see the law court not as a place where private disputes are fought out with legal weapons in front of neutral judges, but as appropriate class-rooms for the judicial education of the masses, so that the courts have an educational as well as a judicial role. But even there it may be doubted whether this would be allowed to lead to injustice and flouting of the law. It may be accepted that incorruptible and impartial judges are generally preferred to corrupt and partial ones.

Participation of ordinary citizens, at least in the form of their presence in open court and criticism in a free press.

This notion expresses the democratic idea that justice belongs to, and concerns, the whole community and not just a limited, highly trained intelligentsia. It also embodies the idea that justice must be seen to be done. Justice in open court is widely prevalent nowadays, whereas the *ancien régime* had a great predilection for *in camera* proceedings and even the secret hearing of witnesses. Yet, even today, the Continent knows the secret inquest by the 'judge of instruction' in preparation for the trial, so that there is no general consensus that all parts of the trial should be public. Moreover, criticism of the judiciary is very risky in England, where contempt of court is a terrible and unpredictable sword of Damocles. Such criticism in the media can be considered contempt of court and punished, even when it is justified.[41] This does not mean, as Lord Parker explained for the Court of Appeal in 1967, that responsible commentary on verdicts and judgments is not permissible, for that freedom is a precious guarantee, but, he added, the emphasis was on responsible comment and it was for the court to decide what 'the limits of responsible comment' were.[42]

Democratic recruitment of judges. That judges should be recruited among persons of character and intelligence without discrimination against any class or ethnic or ideological group is a widely held conviction. The dislike of closed, more or less hereditary judicial castes is widespread, and was one of the reasons for the reaction against the power of the judges at the time of the French Revolution. It must be admitted, however, that this democratic feeling is of a very recent date and that if one takes the 'long duration' as one's time-scale, it is easier to find examples of aristocratic rather than democratic recruitment. In addition, the aristocratic composition of courts of any importance seems to have been accepted by public opinion for many centuries, the feeling being that an aristocrat was born to sit in judgment over ordinary folk and that he would be less likely to succumb to corruption than less wealthy citizens. Although much lip-service is paid to democracy, and the most blatant forms of discrimination in favour of high birth and moneyed or landed wealth have disappeared, the judiciary in western Europe still clearly belongs to well-to-do and educated families and the ordinary working man's son is still a rare bird among the Law Lords or the Courts of Cassation.

Competent and professional judges. This is quickly seen to be a problem. Not, of course, that any one would prefer incompetent to competent judges, but that the criterion of their professionalism is a matter of debate. In some countries all courts – except military, labour and commercial, where lay assessors are active – are manned by law graduates. Elsewhere, as in England, this is by no means the case, for the magistrates hold no law degrees and often no degrees at all. As they sit once or twice a week and may otherwise be absorbed in quite different pursuits – as housewives for example – they cannot be considered professional judges. Yet the system works and leads to few complaints. This leaves only the preference for competent against incompetent judges, which is not much better than a truism.

Comprehensible and cognoscible law. Here consensus may not be difficult to establish. There must be hardly anyone who has a good word to say for the Roman patricians who hid the *formulae* of the law from the vulgar eyes of the plebs in order to safeguard their ascendancy. Everyone now agrees that it is the obvious right of all citizens to know and understand the law and their rights and duties. People are not, or should not be – to use Bentham's well known image – like dogs who only discover that something is forbidden when the stick hits their noses. But as soon as this general statement is left, and the question asked how the law can best be made available and open to everyone, the difficulty starts. Some people think it obvious that a good code and clear and well drafted statutes are the answer to our desideratum. Others, representatives of world famous legal systems, did not and do not think so at all and reject the very idea of codification; they would rather believe in scholars expounding the traditional feeling of the people for justice or in judges carefully observing hallowed precedents and clearly worded statutes (unless they find them unreasonable).[43] It is clear that one is running around in circles. To decide whether legislators', judges', or scholars' law was best, the question was approached as to which law was best, but for that question – insofar as cognoscibility is concerned – reference has to be made back to the role of legislature, judiciary and university. All that is possible here is to admit that there is no agreement in the world, for the great Roman-Germanic and socialist law families so strongly believe in codes that they can hardly imagine life without them, whereas the great and equally world-wide common-law family gets on without codification and prefers it that way. The contrast may not be so sharp in reality for, although the common law has no codes (except for some limited fields), it has an ever increasing amount of legislation to cope with, and some of the most famous continental codes are now so old that much of their substance has been replaced by modern statute law. This statute law has to be interpreted by judges in the daily life of the courts so that case law is of enormous importance in civil-law as well as common-law countries and the cognoscibility of the law depends in both groups to a large extent on the cognoscibility of the relevant cases. It is obvious to any diligent observer that the wish for everyone to be able to know the law is unrealistic and that the Roman law saying 'nemo censetur legem ignorare' (no one is deemed to ignore the law) is pure fiction. It is one of the most blatant legal fictions ever, and at the same time one of the most indispensable, for if the excuse of 'ignorance of the law' were admitted, anyone could get away with anything.

Accessible justice. Here again the agreement on principle should not be difficult to establish: what is the sense of extending various rights to the citizens if the judicial machinery to guarantee their peaceful exercise is defective – because it is too remote in mentality or language, or so long and expensive that winning one's case is more ruinous than giving up one's right? It is evident that the cost of litigation in England in comparison with many other countries is exorbitant so that only people on legal aid or wealthy individuals and companies can afford to go to court. This is a sorry state of affairs, as most people agree, but should one go to the other extreme and make litigation absolutely free? This would be the logical complement of guaranteeing people's rights absolutely, but the practical consequence would probably be the flooding of the courts with *Bagatell-sachen* and the resolve to stop this unrealistic utopia at once. A reasonable contribution to obtain one's right in the courts is the answer, but who will decide what is reasonable? It would not do to make the whole country contribute to a common insurance fund for judicial risks – a sort of 'national law service' – for strangely enough certain parts of various countries are very different in their keenness or proneness to go to court. One is confronted here with a potentially vast field of comparative-historical research, and it seems that very little has been done yet. It is well known that in the twelfth and thirteenth centuries a strikingly high proportion of cases in the English king's courts came from the old Danelaw. In the seventeenth century it was believed that rising prospects led to a rise in litigation.[44] Recent research has discovered some intriguing dissimilarities between various French regions in their degree of litigiousness in the nineteenth century: the discoverer is clearly puzzled himself by what he found and is rather at a loss how to interpret it. How indeed does one explain that there were many more civil cases per thousand inhabitants in the south of France than in the north? Could it be that the southern Roman-law tradition encouraged people to go to court more easily? But how then does one account for the exceptionally high degree of litigation in Normandy, not a Roman-law area but on the contrary one where the very old feudal Norman and Anglo-Norman law and institutions had deep roots? Other explanations such as wealth and political attitudes do not appear to be satisfactory, so where does one turn to explain this puzzling phenomenon?[45] Among historians the English sixteenth century is well known for its high degree of litigiousness,[46] which could have something to do with the country's growing prosperity and urbanisation. These same elements to some extent could account for the fact that at present the United States is reputed to be the most litigious nation in the world, and certainly boasts the highest quota of lawyers per number of inhabitants, i.e. one lawyer per 400 citizens. The political factor, i.e. the supremacy of the law, is, of course, also a powerful contributor to this state of affairs.[47]

Humane justice. If anywhere, here consensus should be easy: who is ever heard clamouring for inhuman justice? No one wants to go back to the evil days of the Inquisition or Stalin's gaols. Regimes that use torture and otherwise flaunt human rights, guaranteed by so many declarations, international treaties and carefully worded constitutions, are rightly condemned by world public opinion. Yet, even here there are snags. The death penalty exists in several countries, while numerous others have abolished it. Many people think it is barbarous and inhuman and the question was even brought before the United States Supreme Court, which had to decide a few years ago whether the death penalty fell under the constitutional ban on 'cruel and unusual punishments' (copied from the English Bill of Rights of 1689).

A legal system based on broad public consent. The law and the courts should be fair to all sections of the people, no group should feel excluded or oppressed. Judicial administration should be on the same wavelength as the country. Should this also mean that the law is made by the people or at least by their representatives? Laws made, or at least accepted, by the people through referendum are today very rare. Laws made by chosen parliaments are more numerous, but some of these parliaments contain chosen representatives who were in fact imposed on the people by the one and only party allowed to exist. What then about the common-law countries, where the core of the legal system was created neither by the people nor by their chosen representatives, but by a venerable priesthood of wise, old, bewigged judges? Here the consent of the country may be considered to manifest itself in the almost universal admiration which the judiciary receives in England, and even beyond the English frontiers. How moreover can abortion laws ever reflect a national consensus when, as opinion polls in some countries show, the proportion of adversaries and supporters is fifty-fifty?

Universally accepted criteria are apparently difficult to find and there is no agreement on some of their concrete aspects. Nevertheless, a great majority of people would find the criteria here enumerated desirable on principle: lack of corruption, participation of the public, access to judicial careers for all deserving individuals, competent judges, cognoscible law, accessible and humane justice and laws, and a judiciary enjoying a broad popular acceptance. How do various countries and periods rate in the light of these criteria? It seems fair at the outset to make a distinction between the centuries before and after the Enlightenment and the modernisation to which it led at various times in various countries – the divide being the codes of Prussia and Austria of 1794 and 1811, the French Revolution, the Napoleonic codes and the English legislation which, after the Reform Bill of 1832, modernised the organisation of the courts (even if it did not alter the common law). The previous centuries, the days of what German historians now like to call the 'Old-European epoch', would certainly not pass our test. The gruesome criminal law and criminal procedure, the obscurity of the law, the terrors of imprisonment for debt, the aristocratic, closed character of the bench (when even J.P.'s were recruited exclusively from the landed classes), the immense length and cost of litigation, particularly in the Church courts and the English Court of Chancery, are just a few of the reasons that come to mind. The question becomes more interesting for the recent past and present and here I propose to scrutinise England, the United States and Western Europe.

England's virtues are obvious: incorruptible judges, the public character of the administration of justice, the participation by the public in the form of the jury, 'reasonable' criticism of the bench and the humane character of the criminal law, without the death penalty or torture (the latter had already disappeared in the seventeenth century). On the shadow side one must point out that the democratic recruitment of the highest judicial bodies seems to be a long way away. They are still clearly a hunting ground for the intellectual elite (against which there is no objection, since one wants the most competent possible judges) and also a social elite. The background of the top of the judiciary is the traditional one of the 'better classes', i.e. public school, Oxford or Cambridge and a father belonging to the liberal professions or the business interest. The twentieth-century judiciary was even more public school oriented than were its predecessors of the eighteenth and nineteenth centuries: of the judges sitting on the bench in 1941 approximately 80% had attended one of the public schools, by 1956 the proportion was 71% and this was unchanged in 1969.[48] A glance at the recent Law Lords and chancellors named in *Part Four: Modern Times 1956–76* of Stevens's *Law and Politics* reveals that of the fourteen Lords mentioned, eight went to Oxford,[49] four to Cambridge,[50] one to Oxford and Edinburgh[51] and one to London and Oxford.[52] A glance at *Whitaker's Almanack 1984*, under *Supreme Judicial Authority*, yielded the name of the Lord Chancellor, Lord Hailsham, who studied at Oxford, the names of nine Lords of Appeal in Ordinary, five of whom studied at Oxford,[53] three at Cambridge[54] and one who had gone to no university but came from a military career.[55] In the Court of Appeal, the Master of the Rolls, Sir John Donaldson, went to Cambridge, and of the eighteen Lords Justices of Appeal, eight went to Oxford,[56] eight to Cambridge,[57] one went to the Royal Military Academy at Woolwich[58] and one went to no university.[59] These figures are quoted by way of example. The reader who wants to pursue the matter can consult the detailed survey in Blom-Cooper and Drewry's work,[60] where, *inter alia*, he will find a column indicating the father's occupation for each of the Law Lords named. There he will meet the law and other liberal professions, some landowners, a fair number of merchants, bank managers and stockbrokers, civil servants, academics and teachers, clerics, two politicians, two brewers, a baker, a printer, a farmer and a soldier.[61] The social background of the magistrates, the successors of the old Justices of the Peace, in general can best be described as educated and well-to-do middle or upper middle-class. The cognoscibility of the law has improved, not only because proceedings are in plain English, but books on the law, written for the general public, try, and generally manage, to explain, on the basis of statutes and cases (which in themselves are not so accessible and often couched in very technical language), what the present state of the law is and what the reasonable prospects are of gaining a particular case. Consent about the existing state of affairs and admiration for the courts are widespread, but the cost of litigation is still a brake on their real accessibility.

In the United States the democratisation of the judicial apparatus has gone much further. This is not only because the whole of American society is more democratic, but also because already in colonial days a tradition of simplicity of the law and easy accessibility of the courts was started, which was part of a general aversion to the more aristocratic and oppressive aspects of seventeenth- and eighteenth-century England.[62] The participation of the public is considerable, not only through the two criminal juries, but also through the election of judges in several states (an effective remedy against caste formation). The length and cost of the litigation tend to be considerable, *inter alia*, because of the numerous degrees of appeal, and the death penalty appears to some as an inhuman punishment. On the whole the judicial organisation seems to be on the same wavelength as the majority of the nation: the role of the Supreme Court in the integration of the black Americans has been conspicuous.

In western Europe in recent times, with the obvious exception of certain periods of aberration,[63] the image of law and the courts is positive. The recruitment of judges is made via university studies which are accessible to all, sometimes followed by more examinations for entry into the judiciary, so that talent and serious work have become decisive factors, rather than financial or social status. The lower ranks of the judiciary, occupied by the magistrates in England, are on the Continent generally occupied by law graduates. Since the law is codified and on principle based on legislation, it is reasonably cognisable, although theoretical works and legal treatises are necessary for the layman who wants to know the relevant case law. The importance of the latter should not be underestimated. The publicity of hearings and the role of the jury – varying from country to country and far from universal – tend to bring justice close to public opinion. The cost of litigation, although real, is far from the dizzying heights horrified continentals hear of in England. On the whole the law is broadly on the same wavelength as public opinion, because legislation in matters that are common-law preserves in England is quite frequent so that new ways of thinking and living can quickly be translated into new, up-to-date statutes. It is only in such sensitive questions as abortion that public opinion can be so divided that Parliament cannot agree what should be done. The disappearance of torture and – *de facto* if not on the statute book – of capital punishment lends a human face to criminal justice, but the inordinate length of remand in custody of accused persons awaiting trial is in certain countries an ugly feature, which many deplore and consider a matter of real urgency. The universal imposition of a statutory maximum, as practised in Scotland, would be a real step forward, as would the generalisation of compensation for innocent suspects who have been held in custody for crimes which they never committed.

NOTES

1 THE COMMON LAW IS DIFFERENT: TEN ILLUSTRATIONS

1 One finds many variants such as *e, ewe, eo, ea, ewa*. See *Handwör-terbuch zur deutschen Rechtsgeschichte*, 1 (Berlin, 1971), col. 1027–30.

2 See F. Liebermann, *Die Gesetze der Angelsachsen*, 11, 1 (Halle, 1906), s.v. *lagu*, pp. 129–30 and s.v. *riht*, p. 184; 11, 2 (1912), s.v. *Gesetz*, pp. 466–71 and s.v. *Recht*, p. 624.

3 The problem has been studied thoroughly by Professor A. K. R. Kiralfy in his paper 'Law and right in English legal history', *La formazione storica del diritto moderno in Europa. Atti del terzo congresso internazionale della Società Italiana di Storia del Diritto*, 111 (Florence, 1977), 1069–86; reprinted in *The Journal of Legal History*, 6 (1985), 49–61.

4 P. De Visscher, *La Constitution Anglaise et le règne de la Loi*, Institut belge des Sciences administratives, Sessions 1945–46 (Brussels, 1946). The author makes clear that he is indeed concerned with 'the rule of law' and Dicey's exposition of it. His lecture is, in fact, a critique of Dicey and in particular of the latter's contention that since in France administrative law exists and not in England, the former country knows no 'rule of law'.

5 L. Cohen-Tanugi, *Le droit sans l'Etat. Sur la démocratie en France et en Amérique* (Paris, 1985), pp. VI, 24.

6 *Democracy in America*, I, p. 286, quoted by D. Duman, *The Judicial Bench in England 1727–1875. The Reshaping of a Professional Elite*, Royal Histor. Soc. Studies in History Series, 29 (London, 1982), p. 102.

7 T. F. T. Plucknett, *A Concise History of the Common Law* (5th ed., London, 1956), p. 54.

8 A. Watson, *The Making of the Civil Law* (Cambridge, Mass., 1981), p. 15.

9 *Ibid.*, p. 19.

10 For a brief but penetrating survey, see G. R. Elton, *English Law in the Sixteenth Century: Reform in an Age of Change*, Selden Society Lecture 1978 (London, 1979).

11 A. Pallister, *Magna Carta. The Heritage of Liberty* (Oxford, 1971), pp. 89–107.

12 T. F. T. Plucknett, 'Bonham's Case and Judicial Review', *Harvard Law Review*, 40 (1927), 30–70.

13 Sir Matthew Hale, *The History of the Common Law of England* (2nd ed., London, 1716), p. 72. The *History* was published post-humously in a first edition in 1713; the author had died in 1676.

14 A new series, *Historians on historians*, was opened at the time of writing by a biography of the great legal historian: G. R. Elton, *F. W. Maitland* (London, 1985).

15 Possibly the most striking example is Radcliffe and Cross, *The English Legal System* (6th ed., by G. J. Hand and D. J. Bentley, London, 1977), whose title seems to promise a survey of the present-day English system, but in fact contains a thorough history of English law from the Anglo-Saxons onwards.

16 Plucknett, *Concise History*, pp. 330, 335 ff.

17 Plucknett, *Concise History*, p. 329, n. 1; H. Hübner, *Kodifikation und Entscheidungsfreiheit des Richters in der Geschichte des Privatrechts*, Beiträge zur neueren Privatrechtsgeschichte. Veröffentlichungen des Instituts für Neuere Privatrechtsgeschichte der Universität zu Köln, 8 (Königstein Ts., 1980), p. 14. The quotations mean: 'it behoves him who makes the law to interpret it' and 'whence the law comes, thence should the interpretation also come'.

18 *Year Books, 33–35 Edward I*, ed. A. J. Horwood, Rolls Series (London, 1874), p. 83, quoted in F. Pollock, *A First Book of Jurisprudence for Students of the Common Law* (6th ed., London, 1929), p. 356: 'Ne glosez point le Statut; nous le savoms meuz de vous, qar nous les feimes.'

19 F. A. R. Bennion, *Statutory Interpretation Codified, with a critical commentary* (London, 1984).

20 Bennion, *Statutory Interpretation*, pp. 226–8.

21 Lord Lloyd of Hampstead, *Introduction to Jurisprudence* (3rd ed., London, 1972), p. 734.

22 M. Radin, 'Statutory Interpretation', *Harvard Law Review*, 43 (1929–30), 871.

23 H. F. Jolowicz, *Lectures on Jurisprudence*, ed. J. A. Jolowicz (London, 1963), p. 290, quotes an example of how a judgment of the

House of Lords produced a result clearly inconsistent with the intention of the Merchant Shipping Act of 1925.

24 Lord Denning, *The Discipline of Law* (London, 1979), pp. 9–22.

25 See W. Friedmann, *Legal Theory* (5th ed., New York, 1967), p. 454.

26 P. Stein, *Legal Institutions. The Development of Dispute Settlement* (London, 1984), p. 92.

27 See on this also G. Williams, *Learning the Law* (7th ed., London, 1963), pp. 101–2; B. Abel-Smith and R. Stevens, *Lawyers and the Courts. A Sociological Study of the English Legal System 1750–1965* (London, 1967), p. 123; A. K. R. Kiralfy, *The English Legal System* (4th ed., London, 1967), pp. 121 ff.

28 R. Munday, 'The common lawyer's philosophy on legislation', *Rechtstheorie*, 14 (1983), 203.

29 T. R. S. Allan, 'Legislative supremacy and the rule of law: democracy and constitutionalism', *Cambridge Law Journal*, 44 (1985), 118.

30 J. W. Gough, *Fundamental Law in English Constitutional History* (Oxford, 1955), p. 2.

31 W. S. Tarnopolsky, *The Canadian Bill of Rights* (2nd ed., Toronto, 1975).

32 See on Dicey: R. A. Cosgrove, *The Rule of Law: Albert Venn Dicey. Victorian Jurist* (Chapel Hill, 1980); T. H. Ford, *Albert Venn Dicey. The Man and his Times* (Chichester, 1985).

33 Pollock, *First Book of Jurisprudence*, p. 357.

34 *The Tudor Constitution. Documents and Commentary* (2nd ed. by G. R. Elton, Cambridge, 1982), p. 238.

35 R. Stevens, *Law and Politics. The House of Lords as a Judicial Body 1800–1976* (London, 1979), p. 409.

36 P. Goodhart, *Referendum* (London, 1971), p. 189.

37 H. W. R. Wade, 'The basis of legal sovereignty', *Cambridge Law Journal* (1955), 174, 182.

38 Allan, 'Legislative supremacy', pp. 111–43.

39 P. S. Atiyah, *Law and Modern Society* (Oxford, 1983), p. 108.

40 Under the title *"Risks" in a Bill of Rights*, *The Times* of 17 July 1985 reported the reaction of Mr Robert Alexander QC to the notion of a British Bill of Rights on the United States' model, intended to enshrine and protect fundamental freedoms. He felt this would run the risk of creating political judges and maintained that there was in the United Kingdom 'neither the consensus to create a new constitutional settlement nor the crisis to compel one'. He also expressed

fears that a Bill of Rights would result in the erosion of Parliament's
supremacy and place the latter in the judges' hands.

41 P. S. Atiyah, *The Rise and Fall of Freedom of Contract* (Oxford, 1979), p. 91.
42 Atiyah, *Rise and Fall*, p. 97.
43 Stevens, *Law and Politics*, p. 37.
44 C. Leitmaier, *Der Katholik und sein Recht in der Kirche. Kritisch-konservative Überlegungen*, Konfrontationen, 10 (Vienna, 1971); P. E. Bolté, *Les droits de l'homme et la papauté contemporaine. Synthèse et textes*, La pensée chrétienne, 1 (Montreal, 1975).
45 Gough, *Fundamental Law*, p. 15.
46 Pallister, *Magna Carta*, p. 101.
47 Gough, *Fundamental Law*, p. 101.
48 *Ibid.*, p. 144.
49 See for the political, doctrinal and historical background of *Marbury v. Madison*, the remarkable analysis by G. L. Haskins, on pp. 182–204 of vol. II: *Foundations of Power: John Marshall, 1801–15* (New York and London, 1981) of the *History of the Supreme Court of the United States*.
50 For a paper and a discussion on the legal arguments for and against judicial review in Belgium: M. Barzin, 'Du contrôle de la constitutionnalité des lois', *Académie Royale de Belgique. Bulletin de la Classe des Lettres et des Sciences Morales et Politiques*, 5th s., 52 (1966), 335–50.
51 J. Gilissen, 'Die belgische Verfassung von 1831 – ihr Ursprung und ihr Einfluss', *Beiträge zur deutschen und belgischen Verfassungsgeschichte im 19. Jahrhundert*, ed. by W. Conze (Stuttgart, 1967), pp. 38–69.
52 F. Pollock, *Essays in Jurisprudence and Ethics* (London, 1882), p. 85.
53 Professor Langbein pointed out also that although the legislature was threatening ever more capital punishment, a declining proportion of persons convicted of felony were actually executed: the 'penal death rate' was declining. See, besides L. Radzinowicz's *History of English Criminal Law and its Administration from 1750*, 4 vols. (London, 1948–68), a recent article by J. H. Langbein, 'Albion's fatal flaws', *Past & Present. A Journal of Historical Studies*, 98 (1983), 96–120.
54 Langbein, 'Albion's fatal flaws', p. 117. S. F. C. Milsom's opinion of the historic criminal law of England is that it was a 'miserable

history' and that 'nothing worthwhile was created' (*Historical Foundations of the Common Law* (2nd ed., London, 1981), p. 403.

55 There exists no European history of criminal law and the national approach, so typical of nineteenth-century historiography, still predominates. Many of these national histories are themselves products of the nineteenth century and, such as J. F. Stephen's *History of the criminal law in England*, 3 vols. (London, 1883), are now out-dated, but not replaced.

56 R. C. van Caenegem, 'Public prosecution of crime in twelfth-century England', *Church and Government in the Middle Ages. Essays presented to C. R. Cheney*, ed. by C. N. L. Brooke *et al.* (Cambridge, 1976), pp. 41–76.

57 For an evaluation see M.-L. Rassat, *Le Ministère public entre son passé et son avenir* (Paris, 1967).

58 At the time of writing a bill is being prepared to stop sending fraud cases before the jury. The reason given by the government is that modern fraud cases are too complex to be grasped by a non-specialist jury. For the same reason certain governments nowadays try to reduce the role of the legislature, because affairs of state have become too complex for the miscellaneous collection of men and women whom the electorate sends to Parliament.

59 See, for Germany: E. Schwinge, *Der Kampf um die Schwurgerichte bis zur Frankfurter Nationalversammlung* (Breslau, 1926) (with an analysis of the developments at the time of the French Revolution); G. Hadding, *Schwurgerichte in Deutschland. Der Schwurgerichtsgedanke seit 1848* (Kassel, 1974). See also the survey by W. R. Cornish, *The Jury* (new ed., Penguin Press, 1971).

60 It is with great interest that we look forward to the results of the work of a group of specialists who have chosen, under the direction of Professor Schioppa, to study the history of the jury on the continent of Europe and in Britain from the eighteenth century onwards. For a preliminary survey, see A. P. Schioppa, 'The Jury', *Englische und kontinentale Rechtsgeschichte: ein Forschungsprojekt*, ed. by H. Coing and K. W. Nörr, Comparative Studies in Continental and Anglo-American Legal History, ed. by H. Coing and K. W. Nörr, 1 (Berlin, 1985), pp. 56–62.

61 The *commorientes*-articles dealt with intestate inheritance and established certain legal presumptions about the order of death of several persons who had died in the same accident (presumptions based on age and sex). See on the civil law origins H. Coing,

Europäisches Privatrecht. I: *Älteres Gemeines Recht (1500 bis 1800)* (Munich, 1985), pp. 203–4.
62 'Judgments should be based on the laws and not on examples', i.e. precedents.
63 K. Zweigert and H. Kötz, *An Introduction to Comparative Law*, transl. T. Weir, II: *The Institutions of Private Law* (Amsterdam, New York, Oxford, 1977), p. 234.
64 In the words of F. Pollock (*First Book of Jurisprudence*, p. 360) 'Francis Bacon put forward in 1616 a carefully considered proposition touching the compiling and amendment of the laws of England. He desired to have a digest of ancient legal rules ... and revised editions of the Statutes and the Yearbooks, omitting obsolete matter. He did not recommend the framing of a new 'text law' – what we should now call a code of the common law: "I dare not advise", he said, "to cast the law into a new mould." '
65 J. A. Colaiaco, *James Fitzjames Stephen and the Crisis of Victorian Thought* (London, 1983), pp. 200–5.
66 J. H. Farrar, *Law Reform and the Law Commission* (London, 1974); R. Cross, *Precedent in English Law* (3rd ed., Oxford, 1977), p. 5.
67 *Commentaries*, adapted by R. M. Kerk, I (London, 1876), p. 41.
68 See Lord Denning's statement in a televised interview on the B.B.C. on 7 November 1982: 'Many lawyers are brought up to believe that the law must be certain, and therefore they must not alter it or develop it in the slightest, it's got to be certain and stay as it is. Even if it does injustice it must be certain. That is the one school of thought. On the other hand there's the school of thought which I would like to represent, namely that it ought to move with the times, and therefore you ought to develop the law, you, if need be, ought to alter old precedents which are bad, in order to bring up the needs for the times.'
69 For the most important recent work on the royal judges in the initial stages of the common law, see D. M. Stenton, *Pleas before the King or his Justices (1198–1212)*, Selden Society 67, 68, 83, 84, 4 vols. (London, 1948–49, 1966–67); R. V. Turner, *The English Judiciary in the Age of Glanvill and Bracton c. 1176–1239* (Cambridge, 1985).
70 For a recent and most thorough survey of this question see S. Kuttner, 'The revival of jurisprudence', *Renaissance and renewal in the twelfth century*, ed. by R. Benson and G. Constable (Cambridge, Mass., 1982), pp. 299–323.
71 See the thorough review of this problem by B. Tierney, ' "The prince

is not bound by the laws." Accursius and the origins of the modern state', *Comparative Studies in Society and History*, 5 (1962), 378–400.

72 C. H. S. Fifoot, *Judge and Jurist in the Reign of Victoria* (London, 1959), p. 21.

73 Cosgrove, *Rule of Law*, p. 52.

74 Fifoot, *Judge and Jurist*, p. 21.

75 *Ibid.*, pp. 24–5. See also the most informative survey by P. Stein, 'Legal theory and the reform of legal education in mid-nineteenth century England', *L'educazione giuridica*. II: *Profili storici*, ed. by A. Giuliani and N. Picardi (Perugia, 1979), pp. 185–206.

76 A. Paterson, *The Law Lords* (London, 1982), p. 15.

2 THE MASTERY OF THE LAW: JUDGES, LEGISLATORS AND PROFESSORS

1 W. Friedmann, *Legal Theory* (5th ed., New York, 1967), p. 210.

2 Roscoe Pound, *The Spirit of the Common Law* (Boston, 1921), pp. 5–6.

3 H. G. Hanbury, *The Vinerian Chair and Legal Education* (Oxford, 1958), Preface.

4 F. H. Lawson, *A Common Lawyer looks at the Civil Law* (Westport, Conn., 1955), p. 46.

5 Art. *Economie politique* in the *Encyclopédie*, 1735, quoted by Cohen-Tanugi, *Le droit sans l'Etat. Sur la démocratie en France et en Amérique* (Paris, 1985), p. XI.

6 J. W. Burrow, *A Liberal Descent. Victorian Historians and the English Past* (Cambridge, 1981), p. 134.

7 'The emperor is not bound by the laws' and 'what has pleased the emperor has force of law'.

8 This acclamation, at the promulgation of the Theodosian Code in 438, was repeated twenty-eight times; at that session sixteen acclamations reached a grand total of 352, as we learn from the *Gesta Senatus Romani de Theodosiano publicando*, in the ed. of the *Codex Theodosianus* by T. Mommsen and P. M. Meyer, I, 2 (Berlin, 1905), pp. 1–4. See D. A. Bullough, 'Games people played: drama and ritual as propaganda in medieval Europe', *Transactions of the Royal Historical Soc.*, 5th s., 24 (1974), 102, who speaks of 'the mindless ritual of repeated acclamation of the emperor', which all too often replaced debate.

9 See, discussing George Lawson who was writing in the mid-seventeenth century, B. Tierney, *Religion, Law, and the growth of Constitutional Thought 1150–1650* (Cambridge, 1982), pp. 97–102. This idea of the 'mixed constitution' was already described by Thomas Aquinas, who wrote in his *Summa theologica*: 'such is any well-mixed polity; [it is mixed] from kingship since there is one at the head of all; from aristocracy in so far as a number of persons are set in authority on account of their virtue; from democracy, and that is the power of the people, in so far as the rulers can be chosen from the people and the people have a right to choose their rulers' (quoted by Tierney, *Religion, Law and Thought*, p. 90).

10 Tennyson quoted in Lord Denning, *The Discipline of Law* (London, 1979), p. 292.

11 The reader is, of course, familiar with the ancient Greek distinction between the monarchic, aristocratic (and oligarchic) and democratic (and demagogic) forms of government. An interesting variant, or transposition adapted to the present time, was formulated by Professor A. Watson in his *The Making of the Civil Law* (Cambridge, Mass., 1981), p. 21, who distinguishes the following three forms: (1) The 'liberal-democratic notion' that 'persons should be treated as formally equal', (2) 'the fascist-aristocratic notion of justice' which 'insists that the inequalities of people should be reflected in the law' and (3) 'the socialist notion of justice' which 'demands that all persons should in law be treated alike, not just formally but in actuality'. I believe that this triad is a useful tool of analysis, but I have my doubts about the junction of 'fascist' and 'aristocratic', which ignores the plebeian element in fascism.

12 On Hale, see E. Heward, *Matthew Hale* (London, 1972) and on the law reform, G. B. Nourse, 'Law reform under the commonwealth and protectorate', *Law Quarterly Review*, 75 (1959), 519–29, and M. Cotterell, 'Interregnum law reform: the Hale Commission of 1652', *English Historical Review*, 83 (1968), 689–704.

13 As one historian put it: 'advocacy of law reform had become closely associated with attacks on property rights' (W. Prest, 'The English Bar 1550–1700', *Lawyers in Early Modern Europe and America*, ed. by W. Prest (London, 1981), p. 76). And another writes that as the common people were drawn more and more into politics 'so the demand for legal reform had become a demand for social reform, for protection of the middling and poorer sort' (C. Hill, *Intellectual Origins of the English Revolution* (Oxford, 1965), p. 263). For the

whole episode one may consult D. Veall, *The Popular Movement for Law Reform 1640–1660* (Oxford, 1970).

14 H. E. Troje, *Europa und griechisches Recht* (Frankfurt, 1971). Troje's argument is that both the Athenian democracy and the Byzantine absolutism went contrary to the aristocratic constitution of classical Rome and feudal Europe. See on the laws of the Athenians, *inter alia*, R. J. Bonner and G. Smith, *The Administration of Justice from Homer to Aristotle* (Chicago, 1930); A. R. W. Harrison, *The Law of Athens*, II: *Procedure* (Oxford, 1971).

15 W. Ullmann, 'This realm of England is an empire', *Journal of Ecclesiastical History*, 30 (1979), 175–203.

16 It was around the middle of the seventeenth century that two important Greek law-texts were published, a reconstruction of the so called *Leges Atticae* (with an extensive commentary) and the complete *Basilica* (Troje, *Europa*, p. 17). Whereas Greek law was surely democratic in its procedure, allowing for courts with large numbers of lay judges, its weakness, from a democratic point of view, was its poor cognoscibility, since its content could not be found in official, or even unofficial collections, and had to be discovered mainly from speeches and such material.

17 R. C. van Caenegem, 'Le droit romain en Belgique', *Ius Romanum Medii Aevi*, ed. by F. Genzmer, v, 5, b (Milan, 1966), p. 47.

18 It could, and to a large extent did, fall into the hands of another guild, that of the practitioners of the law, the serjeants and the senior judges who were selected from their ranks. See for the role of this guild instinct among English lawyers the introduction by O. Kahn-Freund in K. Renner, *The Institutions of Private Law and their Social Functions*, Internat. Library of Sociology and Social Reconstruction, ed. by K. Mannheim (London, 1949), pp. 12–13: 'English law evolved as a series of guild rules for the use and guidance of the members and apprentices of the Inns of Court. It was due to political factors, to the failure of absolute monarchy in England . . . that the administration of the law remained in the hands of the lawyers' guilds.'

19 W. Stubbs, *Select Charters and other illustrations of English Constitutional History* (9th ed. by H. W. C. Davis, Oxford, 1913), pp. 161–89.

20 See the remarks of Lord Wilberforce in the televised interview of Lord Denning, broadcast by the B.B.C. on 7 November 1982.

21 See, however, the optimistic noises in J. N. Hazard, *Managing*

Change in the USSR. The politico-legal role of the Soviet Jurist, Goodhart Lectures 1982 (Cambridge, 1983).

22 A. Paterson, *The Law Lords* (London, 1982), pp. 10–15. It is pleasant to note that two Law Lords made an express exception for criticisms formulated by Professor A. L. Goodhart, whose name was given to the present lectures (*Ibid.*, pp. 17 and 19).

23 The classic work is J. Bonnecase, *L'Ecole de l'Exégèse en Droit Civil* (Paris, 1924). See also a recent doctoral dissertation in the University of Ghent: B. Bouckaert, *De exegetische school. Een kritische studie van de rechtsbronnen– en interpretatieleer bij de 19de eeuwse commentatoren van de Code Civil* (Antwerp, 1981).

24 See on all this: J.-P. Royer, *La société judiciaire depuis le XVIIIe siècle* (Paris, 1979), pp. 209–62.

25 A. J. Arnaud, *Essai d'analyse structurale du Code Civil français. La Règle du Jeu dans la Paix Bourgeoise* (Paris, 1973).

26 Clause 17 of Magna Carta, ruling that 'common pleas shall not follow our court, but shall be held in some certain place', has been understood for centuries as establishing the Court of Common Pleas at Westminster. Recently, however, it has been argued that this 'certain place' only came to refer to Westminster late in the thirteenth century: M. T. Clanchy, 'Magna Carta and the common pleas', *Studies in medieval history presented to R. H. C. Davis*, ed. by H. Mayr-Harting and R. I. Moore (London, 1985), pp. 219–32.

27 J. H. Baker, *The Order of Serjeants at Law. A chronicle of creations, with related texts and a historical introduction*, Selden Society Supplementary Series, 5 (London, 1984).

28 See on the need to break occasionally with *stare decisis*: Lord Denning, *The Discipline of Law*, p. 287.

29 Paterson, *Law Lords*, p. 14, quotes Lord Radcliffe as saying that the 'judge should not be too outspoken about his legislative role. A judge who is seen to be developing the law runs the risk of undermining his authority by revealing that on occasions he acts as a legislator without democratic authority' and he went on to say (quotation on p. 142): 'If a judge of reasonable strength of mind thought a particular precedent wrong, he must be a great fool if he couldn't get round it.'

30 Pound, *The Spirit*, p. 46.

31 H. F. Jolowicz, *Lectures on Jurisprudence*, ed. J. A. Jolowicz (London, 1963), p. 290.

32 It seems superfluous to refer to the well known English authorities on

Coke, but it may be useful to draw attention to a French mono-
graph of real merit: J. Beauté, *Un grand juriste anglais: Sir Edward
Coke 1552–1634. Ses idées politiques et constitutionnelles* (Paris,
1975).

33 See A. W. B. Simpson, 'The common law and legal theory', *Oxford
Essays in Jurisprudence, second series*, ed. by A. W. B. Simpson
(Oxford, 1973), pp. 89–91. Cf. H. L. A. Hart, *The Concept of Law*
(London, 1961), p. 132 and the critical appraisal of *stare decisis* by
D. Kairys, 'Legal reasoning', *The Politics of Law. A Progressive
Critique*, ed. by D. Kairys (New York, 1982), pp. 11–17.

34 R. A. Cosgrove, *The Rule of Law: Albert Venn Dicey – Victorian
Jurist* (Chapel Hill, 1980), p. 25, quoting A. V. Dicey, 'The Study of
Jurisprudence', *Law Magazine and Review*, 4th s., 5 (August 1880),
382.

35 Stevens, *Law and Politics. The House of Lords as a Judicial Body
1800–1976* (London, 1979), p. 194.

36 P. S. Atiyah, *Law and Modern Society* (Oxford, 1983), p. 1.

37 I noticed with interest that the author of a recent book on American
and French democracy also seems to think of American judicial
power as being caused by the failings (*la carence*) of the federal
legislative and executive organs. See Cohen-Tanugi, *Le droit sans
l'Etat*, p. 84.

38 See the remarks in J. Gilissen, *Introduction historique au droit*
(Brussels, 1979), pp. 265–7.

39 J. H. Shennan, *The Parlement of Paris* (London, 1968), pp.
285–325; Royer, *Société judiciaire*, pp. 123–66.

40 The first line of the *Vorbemerkung* in Professor H. Coing's new and
fundamental book on the history of European private law baldly
states that 'Rechtsgeschichte ist ein Teil der *Kulturgeschichte*'
(author's italics) and explains, referring to J. Burckhardt, that it is
the task of legal history to describe people's mode of thought and
views (*Denkweise und Anschauungen*) in a period of the past:
Europäisches Privatrecht, I, p. 1.

41 The reader is reminded of the writings of Rudolf von Jhering (died
1892), particularly his *Kampf ums Recht* (1872): see F. Wieacker,
Privatrechtsgeschichte der Neuzeit (2nd ed., Göttingen, 1967), pp.
450–53. That power politics dominate the law and that 'justice or
right is simply what is in the interest of the stronger party' was
already the position of Thrasymachus in Part I of Plato's *Republic*
(transl. D. Lee, 2nd ed., Penguin Press, 1974), p. 77. See K. Mino-

gue's review of J. A. G. Griffith, *The Politics of the Judiciary*, in *Times Literary Supplement*, 6 January 1978, p. 11.

42 Judgment should be given on the basis of laws and not examples, i.e. precedents.

43 An authoritative but brief survey will now be found in G. Dolezalek and K. W. Nörr, 'Die Rechtsprechungssammlungen der mittelalterlichen Rota', *Handbuch der Quellen und Literatur der neueren europäischen Privatrechtsgeschichte. 1. Mittelalter (1100–1500). Die gelehrten Rechte und die Gesetzgebung*, ed. by H. Coing (Munich, 1973), pp. 849–56. This can be complemented by G. Dolezalek, 'Die handschriftliche Verbreitung von Rechtsprechungssammlungen der Rota', *Zeitschrift der Savigny-Stiftung für Rechtsgeschichte*, K.A., 58 (1972), 1–104.

3 THE DIVERGENT PATHS OF COMMON LAW AND CIVIL LAW

1 H. J. Berman, *Law and Revolution. The Formation of the Western Legal Tradition* (Cambridge, Mass., 1983), pp. 413 ff., gives an excellent account of this 'first modern territorial state in the West'.

2 G. J. Hand, *English Law in Ireland 1290–1324*, Cambridge Studies in English Legal History (Cambridge, 1967).

3 Decretals of Gregory IX, book 1, title iv, ch. iii, cf. J. P. Dawson, *A History of Lay Judges* (Cambridge, Mass., 1960), p. 66. The decretal did not deal with the jury *stricto sensu*, but with the active participation of unlearned people in litigation and judgment finding.

4 C. Donahue and N. Adams, *Select Cases from the Ecclesiastical Courts of the Province of Canterbury c. 1200–1301*, Selden Society, 95 (London, 1981).

5 W. Ullmann, 'This realm of England is an empire', *Journal of Ecclesiastical History*, 30 (1979).

6 G. R. Elton, *F. W. Maitland* (London, 1985), pp. 79–88.

7 E. Heward, *Matthew Hale* (London, 1972), p. 26. The author explains Hale's admiration for Roman law because of his scientific turn of mind. He maintains that Hale's knowledge of Roman law and its methods of arrangement provided the background for his attempt to classify the common law in his *The Analysis of the Law*.

8 The importance of the political factor was stressed by O. Kahn-Freund, who wrote that 'with some exaggeration one might say that it was the Revolution of 1688, not the refusal to 'receive' Roman law that, in this country, sealed the fate of systematic legal science in the

continental sense' (in his Introduction to K. Renner, *The Institutions of Private Law and their Social Functions*, Internat. Library of Sociology and Social Reconstruction, ed. by K. Mannheim (London, 1949), pp. 12–13). It may indeed be held that the fate of the civilians was sealed by the ultimate victory of the anti-absolutist party, but it should not be forgotten that in the mid-seventeenth century the party of the Puritan reformers had broken its teeth on the stubborn resistance of the common lawyers. The latter's guild had resisted the attacks both of the royalists and of the Puritans.

9 I quote the translation by D. Ogg, *Johannis Seldeni Ad Fletam Dissertatio*. Reprinted from the edition of 1647 with parallel translation, introduction and notes, Cambridge Studies in English Legal History (Cambridge, 1925), p. 165. As examples of this national 'aversion' Selden quotes King Stephen's edict against Vacarius, Henry III's ban on London law schools and the famous *Nolumus mutare leges Angliae* of the barons at Merton. Selden also uses the term 'reception' for the spread of Roman law in Europe in the twelfth century ('. . . ita jam receptum fuisse juris Justinianei usum', p. 96) and points out in that context that Roman law was not introduced by decree but because of its own intrinsic quality ('rationis juridicae promptuarium optimum ac ditissimum').

10 D. T. Oliver, 'Roman law in modern cases in English courts', *Cambridge Legal Essays in Honour of Doctor Bond, Professor Buckland and Professor Kenny* (Cambridge, 1926), pp. 243–57. The author quotes on p. 246 the following saying from Tindal CJ in *Acton* v. *Blundell* (1843): 'The Roman law forms no rule, binding in itself upon the subject of these realms; but, in deciding a case upon principle, where no direct authority can be cited from our books, it affords no small evidence of the soundness of the conclusion at which we have arrived, if it proves to be supported by that law, the fruits of the researches of the most learned men, the collective wisdom of ages and the groundwork of the municipal law of most of the countries in Europe.'

11 Zweigert and Kötz, *Introduction*, 1: *The Framework* (Amsterdam, New York, Oxford, 1977), p. 148.

12 W. Seagle, *The Quest of Law* (New York, 1941); R. Dekkers, *Le droit privé des peuples. Caractères, destinées, dominantes* (Brussels, 1953); J. Gilissen, *Introduction historique au droit* (Brussels, 1979).

13 A. Guzmán, *Ratio Scripta*, Ius Commune. Veröffentlichungen des

Max-Planck-Instituts für Europäische Rechtsgeschichte, Sonderhefte. Texte und Monographien, 14 (Frankfurt, 1981).

14 F. H. Lawson, *A Common Lawyer Looks at the Civil Law* (Westport, Conn., 1955), p. 63.

4 WHICH IS BEST, CASE LAW, STATUTE LAW OR BOOK LAW?

1 H. F. Jolowicz, *Lectures on Jurisprudence*, ed. J. A. Jolowicz
(London, 1963), p. 180.

2 If change there had to be, it was for the legislator to bring it about.
See, for example, a pronouncement by Lord Cohen: 'Uncertainty in
the law is a supreme disadvantage and if we abandon the principle of
stare decisis we open the door wide to uncertainty. I think there is
much to be said for a rule which prevents the judiciary from usurping
the function of the legislature and tends to certainty in the law'
(A. Paterson, *The Law Lords* (London, 1982), p. 133). Hence,
although he considered that the decision of *Simonin* v. *Mallac* of
1860 was wrong, Lord Cohen declined to overrule it because it had
stood for over a hundred years and had been followed or applied in a
large number of cases in England and the Commonwealth (*Ibid.*,
p. 136).

3 John Vaughan, Chief Justice of the Common Pleas from 1668 to
1674, in *Bole* v. *Horton*, 1673, quoted in C. K. Allen, *Law in the
Making* (7th ed., Oxford, 1964), pp. 209–10. A similar feeling had
been expressed centuries earlier by Jacobus Butrigarius (1274–
1348), who wrote: 'Nota quod judex non debet sequi sententias, nisi
in se habeant rationem', i.e. a judge should not follow precedents
unless they are reasonable (*In codicis libros commentaria*, ad lib. 7,
tit. 45, 1. 13, quoted by A. Guzmán, *Ratio scripta*, Ius Commune.
Veröffentlichungen des Max-Planck-Instituts für Europäische
Rechtsgeschichte, Sonderhefte. Texte und Monographien, 14
(Frankfurt, 1981), p. 56).

4 Lord Denning, *The Discipline of Law* (London, 1979), pp. 287–313;
Paterson, *The Law Lords* (London, 1982), pp. 149–50. See also
Lord Denning's views expressed in the televised interview, broadcast
by the B.B.C. on 7 November 1982.

5 R. Stevens, *Law and Politics. The House of Lords as a Judicial Body
1800–1976* (London, 1979), p. 490.

6 H. van den Brink, *The Charm of Legal History* (Amsterdam, 1974),
p. 51. This famous passage (*Il.* XVIII, 497 ff.) bristles with difficulties

and has been the object of many discussions. The reader will find a brief and balanced account of the problems involved in R. J. Bonner and G. Smith, *The Administration of Justice from Homer to Aristotle* (Chicago, 1930), pp. 30–41.

7 J. P. Dawson, *A History of Lay Judges* (Cambridge, Mass., 1960), pp. 137–45 explains the origin of the appointment of local gentry to the commissions of the peace and shows that the J.P.s assumed their burdensome public duties as an inescapable consequence of their own wealth and social position. He estimates that in 1689 there were about 3,000 justices commissioned, of whom perhaps 700 to 800 were active. To what extent being a J.P. was a question of status was shown in 1833 when the J.P.s of a certain county went on strike because someone had been made a J.P. who had been a shopkeeper and was a Methodist.

8 J. P. Dawson, *The Oracles of the Law* (Ann Arbor, 1968), p. 2. See further revealing figures in P. Stein, 'Safety in numbers: sharing of responsibility for judicial decision in early modern Europe', *Diritto e Potere nella Storia Europea. Atti in onore di B. Paradisi*, I (Florence, 1982), pp. 271–83 (Quarto Congresso Internat. Soc. It. di Storia del Diritto).

9 D. Duman, *The Judicial Bench in England 1727–1825. The Reshaping of a Professional Elite*, Royal Histor. Soc. Studies in History Series, 29 (London, 1982), p. 17.

10 R. C. van Caenegem, *Les arrêts et jugés du Parlement de Paris sur appels flamands conservés dans les registres du Parlement*, I: *Textes (1320–1453)*, II: *Textes (1454–1521)*, Receuil de l'ancienne jurisprudence de la Belgique, 1ᵉ série (Brussels, 1966–77).

11 For Europe see: F. Ranieri 'Vom Stand zum Beruf. Die Professionalisierung des Juristenstandes als Forschungsaufgabe der europäischen Rechtsgeschichte der Neuzeit', *Ius Commune. Veröffentlichungen des Max-Planck-Instituts für Europäische Rechtsgeschichte*, 13 (1985), 83–105. For England: C. W. Brooks, 'The common lawyers in England, c. 1558–1642', *Lawyers in Early Modern Europe and America*, ed. by W. Prest (London, 1981), pp. 42–64, and W. Prest, 'The English Bar', pp. 65–85. Admissions to the four Inns of Court increased steadily from perhaps around fifty per year in the early sixteenth century to a high point of 300 in the later years of James I (Brooks, 'The Common Lawyers', p. 53). The Inns became more popular than ever as fashionable finishing schools for the sons of the nobility and the gentry (p. 54). The exclusion orders of 1614

declared that the purpose of the Inns was to provide for the education of the nobility and gentry of the realm (p. 54). The admissions registers of the Inns of Court indicate that between 1590 and 1640 as many as 88% of entrants were members of the gentry (p. 56), although one should realise that the term 'gentleman' came to be used less strictly in the early seventeenth century. Prest, 'The English Bar', p. 79 writes that before the civil war the Inns of Court had flourished as 'liberal academies for the gentry'.

12 C. Schott, 'Wir Eidgenossen fragen nicht nach Bartole und Balde', *Gerichtslauben-Vorträge. Freiburger Festkolloquium zum fünfundsiebzigsten Geburtstag von Hans Thieme*, ed. by K. Kroeschell (Sigmaringen, 1983), pp. 17–45.

13 Dawson, *Oracles*, p. 250.

14 D. Dakin, 'The breakdown of the Old Régime in France', *The New Cambridge Modern History*, VIII, ed. by A. Goodwin (Cambridge, 1971), p. 596.

15 J.-P. Royer, *La Société judiciaire depuis le XVIIIe siècle* (Paris, 1979), p. 210. The personnel of the Parlements belonged for about 90% to the nobility before they bought their offices, and their letters of nobility were checked by the councillors upon their admission. This was an even more stringent requirement than a law degree, so the term *aristocratie thémistique* was quite appropriate.

16 Two unsuccessful attempts to return to an elective judiciary were undertaken, in 1848, in the republican zeal of that revolutionary year, and in 1882, when the Third Republic felt that the judiciary was too conservative and thought that the electorate might return more republican-feeling judges (Royer, *Société judiciaire*, pp. 245–48). It was in those years that references to elective judges in the United States caused hilarity in the French Parliament (A. Desjardins, 'La magistrature élue', *Revue des Deux Mondes*, 52, pp. 549–75).

17 Royer, *Société judiciaire*; J. Poumarède, 'La Magistrature et la République. Le débat sur l'élection des juges en 1882', *Mélanges P. Hébraud* (Toulouse, 1981), pp. 665–81; P. Lecocq and R. Martinage, 'Les magistrats et la politique au XIXe siècle. L'exemple des commissions mixtes de 1852', *The Legal History Review*, 50 (1982), 19–47; R. Martinage, J.-P. Royer and P. Lecocq, *Juges et Notables au XIXe siècle* (Paris, 1982); P. Lecocq and R. Martinage, 'L'inamovibilité de la magistrature française dans les constitutions au XIXe siècle et son application', *Liber Amicorum John Gilissen* (Antwerp,

1983), 215–48; R. Martinage, 'Splendeurs et misères de l'inamovibilité de la Magistrature française du XIXe siècle', *Handelingen VIIIe Belgisch-Nederlands Rechtshistorisch Colloquium*, ed. by M. Magits (Antwerp, 1984), pp. 99–118.

18 The students at the Inns, who 'were the sons of the best or better sort of gentlemen of all the shires of England' and 'ought to be gentlemen and that of three descents at least' had to pay considerable sums for their education, and King James I made an order that no one was to be admitted to an Inn of Court that was not a gentleman by descent. See on all this D. Veall, *The Popular Movement for Law Reform 1640–1660* (Oxford, 1970), pp. 30–64; Brooks, 'The Common Lawyers', pp. 42–64; Prest, 'The English Bar', pp. 65–85.

19 The president of one of the chambers of the Royal Court at Montpellier wanted to become first president and wrote, in 1823, to his protector. He mentioned as his foremost merit the fact that he lived in the finest house of Montpellier (in fact, the old Palace of the Estates of Languedoc) and that he had an income of 200,000 francs per year in rents (Royer, *Société judiciaire*, p. 283).

20 L. Prosdocimi, 'Chierici e laici nella società occidentale del secolo XII. A prososito di Decr. Grat. C. 12 q. 1 c. 7: "Duo sunt genera Christianorum"', *Proceedings of the Second International Congress of Medieval Canon Law. Boston College 12–16 August 1963*, ed. by S. Kuttner and J. J. Ryan, Vatican, 1965, pp. 105–22 (Monumenta Iuris Canonici. Series C: Subsidia, 1).

21 J. Langbein, *Torture and the Law of Proof. Europe and England in the Ancien Régime* (Chicago, 1976).

22 Since elective judges nowadays occur mainly in the United States, some American bibliography may be useful here. *Judicial Selection and Tenure. Selected Readings*, ed. by G. R. Winters (2nd ed., Chicago, 1973); S. S. Escovitz, *Judicial Selection and Tenure*, The American Judicature Society (Chicago, 1975); 'Judicial Selection in the states: a critical study with proposals for reform', *Hofstra Law Review*, 4 (Winter 1976), 267–353.

23 The cluster of problems around the ascending and descending themes of government was first expounded by W. Ullmann in a review of a book by M. J. Odenheimer in the *Revue d'Histoire du Droit*, 26 (1958), 360–66. See W. Ullmann, *Law and Politics in the Middle Ages. An Introduction to the Sources of Medieval Political Ideas*, The Sources of History: Studies in the Uses of Historical Evidence (London, 1975), pp. 30 ff.

24 H. J. Berman, *Law and Revolution: The Formation of the Western legal tradition* (Cambridge, Mass. 1983), p. 429.
25 R. C. van Caenegem and L. Milis, 'Kritische uitgave van de "Grote Keure" van Filips van de Elzas, graaf van Vlaanderen, voor Gent en Brugge (1165–1177)', *Handelingen Koninklijke Commissie voor Geschiedenis*, 143 (1977), 238.
26 See J. Gilissen, *Le régime représentatif avant 1790 en Belgique*, Coll. 'Notre Passé' (Brussels, 1952), pp. 29–50.
27 Dawson, *Oracles*, p. 281.
28 Stevens, *Law and Politics*, pp. 33–4. The position of the Law Lords was confirmed by the Appellate Jurisdiction Act of 1876.
29 Indeed the councillors in the Courts of Appeal are appointed from two lists with two candidates, one submitted by the Court itself and one by the Provincial Council; the councillors in the Court of Cassation are appointed from two lists with two candidates, one submitted by the Court itself and one by the Senate).
30 The highest appointments, Lords of Appeal in Ordinary, Lords Justices and Heads of Division are made on the recommendation of the Prime Minister, after consultation with the Lord Chancellor, who is responsible for the other judicial appointments, from the High Court and Circuit Judges downwards. The Lord Chancellor seeks the feeling of the professional community and in so doing attaches great importance to the views of members of the bar and the bench.
31 See the observations of Roscoe Pound, *The Spirit of the Common Law* (Boston, 1921), p. 57.
32 See the remarks by L. Cohen-Tanugi, *Le droit sans l'Etat. Sur la démocratie en France et en Amérique* (Paris, 1985), p. 55.
33 Pound, *The Spirit*, p. 47.
34 G. L. Haskins, 'De la codification du droit en Amérique du Nord au XVIIe siècle: une étude de droit comparé', *Revue d'Histoire du Droit*, 23 (1955), 311–32; G. L. Haskins, *Law and Authority in Early Massachusetts* (New York, 1960).
35 F. Whyte, *For the Sacred Law of the Land*, 28 November 1652, quoted by Veall, *Popular Movement for Law Reform*, p. 65.
36 P. Classen, *Studium und Gesellschaft im Mittelalter*, ed. by J. Fried, Schriften der Monumenta Germaniae Historica, 29 (Stuttgart, 1983), p. 27.
37 Brooks, 'The common lawyers', p. 59.
38 See, among recent studies, G. Marini (ed.), *A. F. J. Thibaut–F. C.*

Savigny. La polemica sulla codificazione (Naples, 1982); G. Dilcher and B.-R. Kern, 'Die juristische Germanistik des 19. Jahrhunderts und die Fachtradition der deutschen Rechtsgeschichte', *Zeitschrift der Savigny-Stiftung für Rechtsgeschichte, G.A.*, 100 (1984), 1–46. Savigny knew success in conservative circles in the United Kingdom, where the first English translation of his *Vom Beruf unsrer Zeit für Gesetzgebung und Rechtswissenschaft* was published in 1831. His arguments were eagerly taken up by English opponents of codification. See J. R. Dinwiddy, 'Early-nineteenth-century reactions to Benthamism', *Transactions Royal Histor. Soc.*, 5th s., 34 (1984), 56–9.

39 *Collected Papers*, I (Cambridge, 1911), pp. 476–7.

40 Dawson, *Oracles*, p. 386.

41 P. O'Higgins, *Censorship in Britain* (London, 1972), p. 40, referring to a case involving the editor of the *New Statesman* in 1928.

42 O'Higgins, *Censorship*, p. 41.

43 See the situation in the days of Sir Edward Coke. If a judge did not like a previous judgment, he could dismiss it as 'a sudden opinion' or he could find a later precedent 'fitter for the modern practice of the law'. If he did not like a statute he could appeal to custom or 'common right and reason' or he could construe it by 'the rule and reason of the common law' (C. Hill, *Intellectual Origins of the English Revolution* (Oxford, 1965), pp. 251–2, who talks of 'this mysterious process').

44 Thus Sir Edward Coke: 'Peace is the mother of plenty – and plenty the nurse of suits' (IV Institutes, p. 76, quoted in Hill, *Intellectual Origins*, p. 227). In the same sense: Bacon, *Works*, XIII, p. 64, quoted by Hill, *Intellectual Origins*, p. 250. One historian talks of a 'spectacular increase in the volume of civil litigation and other opportunities for common lawyers during the middle decades of the sixteenth century' (Prest, 'The English Bar', p. 66); another writes: 'There was an enormous increase in central court litigation between 1560 and 1640. Business in King's Bench increased by a factor of four between 1560 and 1580 and the number of cases which reached advanced stages in these courts more than doubled again between 1580 and 1640' (Brooks, *The Common Lawyers*, p. 52).

45 B. Schnapper, 'Pour une géographie des mentalités judiciaires: la litigiosité en France au XIXe siècle', *Annales, Economies. Sociétés. Civilisations*, 34 (1979), 399–419. Another historian, studying the recruitment of judges in nineteenth-century France, finds that in

some regions applicants for judicial functions were easily found. This was the case in Normandy, for example, 'because of the abundance of rich lawyers and the wealth from agriculture': judges were badly paid and people without independent means less likely to come forward for judicial posts. Could there be a connection between high litigiousness and an abundance of well-to-do lawyers in a region of 'richesse agricole'? See Royer, *Société judiciaire*, p. 254.

46 Prest, 'The English Bar', p. 67, writes that 'it appears that there were more barristers in private practice per head of population in England and Wales during the early seventeenth century than there are today': the highest recorded total to date of calls to the bar was in the year of the Restoration (*Ibid.*, p. 77).

47 Cohen-Tanugi, *Le droit sans l'Etat*, p. 133.

48 Duman, *The Judicial Bench in England*, p. 41.

49 Lords Kilmuir, Dilhorne, Gardiner, Hailsham, Radcliffe, Denning, Wilberforce and Diplock.

50 Lords Devlin, Reid, Simon and Salmon.

51 Lord Kilbrandon.

52 Lord Edmund-Davies.

53 Lords Diplock, Fraser of Tullybelton, Keith of Kinkel, Scarman and Roskill. Lord Keith of Kinkel also went to Edinburgh.

54 Lords Brandon of Oakbrook, Brightman and Templeman.

55 Lord Bridge of Harwich.

56 Stephenson, Eveleigh, O'Connor, Fox, May, Slade, Goff and Dillon, LL.JJ.

57 Lawton, Waller, Hovell-Thurlow-Cumming-Bruce, Ackner, Oliver, Griffiths, Kerr, Purchas, LL.JJ.

58 Lord Justice Dunn.

59 T. Watkins. I based my research on *Who's Who*, 1985.

60 L. Blom-Cooper and G. Drewry, *Final Appeal. A Study of the House of Lords in its Judicial Capacity* (Oxford, 1972), pp. 160–63: *Law Lords in Action 1952–1968*.

61 I am grateful to Lord Dacre, Master of Peterhouse, who gave me practical help for the compilation of this information.

62 See in particular the Massachusetts Code of 1648: Haskins, *Law and Authority*.

63 E. Kern, *Geschichte des Gerichtsverfassungsrechts* (Munich, Berlin, 1954), c. 7: *Das deutsche Gerichtsverfassungsrecht unter der Herrschaft des Nationalsozialismus*, pp. 197–283.

INDEX

abortion, 31, 158, 164, 168
abridgment, 79
absolutism 37, 39, 49, 73, 79, 83, 92,
  119, 122, 177 n.18; Byzantine, 177
  n.14; enlightened, 49;
  parliamentary, 22, 26
Accursius, 56
accusation, criminal, 4
Achilles, 132
Ackner, D. J. C., 188 n.57
action, 94, 98
adaptation, 7, 96
adjudication, 110, 111, 126, 128,
  130, 133, 135
administration, 82, 93, 110; urban,
  132
advocate, 34, 35, 95
Advocate General, 29
Æ, æw, 3, 4; folces 3
agora, 76, 83
aid, legal, 78, 162
Aktenversendung, 64
Alciatus, A., 58
aldermen, 117, 136; appointed, 131,
  148; co-opted, 148; elected, 131
Alexander I, tsar, 52
Alexander III, pope, 110
Alexander Robert, 171 n.40
Alfonso X, king of Castile, 59
Alfred the Great, king of England, 3,
  93
Allgemeines Landrecht für die
  Preussischen Staaten, 50
Allgemeiner Teil, 32
American Bar Association, 151
anatomy, 89
Anglomania, 123
Anglo-Saxon, 54, 170 n.15
Antigone, 30

Antiqui, 90
Antiquity, 57, 82; Germanic 132
appeal, 4, 104, 109, 136, 142, 149,
  167; absence of, 5; aversion from,
  5; different meanings of, 4;
  introduction of, 6
Appellate Jurisdiction Act, 186 n.28
Aquinas, Thomas, 176 n.9
aristocracy, 52, 76, 78, 108, 140,
  141, 145, 146, 159, 160, 165, 167,
  176 n.9, 176 n.11, 177 n.14
aristocratie thémistique, 140, 184
  n.15
Arnold, C., 138
articles, 121
asetnysse, 3, 4
asettan, 3
assembly, of freemen, 147; legislative,
  152; representative, 107;
  revolutionary, 91
assessor, lay, 160
Athelstan, king of England, 4
Athens, 76, 81–83, 177 n.14
Atiyah, P. S., 24
Attorney General, 5, 48
Austin, J., 99
Austria, 155, 165
authoritarianism, 73, 75, 82
authority, 125, 126, 128, 131, 138,
  148, 178 n.29, 181 n.10; apostolic,
  109, 130; central, 109, 110;
  democratic, 178 n.29; imperial,
  126; judicial, 151; legal, 42, 103;
  royal, 6, 100; of the state, 34
autocracy, 73–75, 80, 92, 156, 157
Azo, 56, 97

Bacon, Francis, 22, 45, 155, 174
  n.64, 187 n.44

189

Index

despotism, enlightened, 49; oriental, 73
Devlin, Lord, 188 n. 50
Dicey, A. V., 22, 62, 169 n. 4, 171 n. 32, 179 n. 34
dictatorship, elective, 23
Digest, 12, 54, 55, 122
digest of laws, 174 n. 64
Dilhorne, Lord, 188 n. 49
Dillon, G. B. H., 188 n. 56
Diplock, Lord, 188 n. 49 and n. 53
Director of Public Prosecutions, 35
diritto, 2
discipline, intellectual, 158
discretion, judicial, 153
discrimination, 152, 159, 160
disinheritance, 131
disputation, 126
dispute settlement, 74, 131, 132, 158
divorce, 2
doctrine, legal, 60, 89, 93, 99, 101, 107, 111, 145, 157
dom, 3, 4
Domat, Jean, 70
Dominate, 73
Donaldson, John, 166
dooms, Old-English, 95
Dorna, Bernard de, 6
droit, 2, 3
droit, ancien, 8, 11
droit commun, 44; *français*, 107; *intermédiaire*, 11, 43, 156; *nouveau*, 8
Dumoulin, Ch., 60, 70, 106, 107
Dunn, R. H. W., 188 n. 58
Durantis, William, 6
duty, 153, 158
dynasty, 15

Ecole de Magistrature, 63
Edinburgh, 166, 188 n. 53
Edmund-Davies, Lord, 188 n. 52
education, 158
Edward I, king of England, 8, 85, 95
Eldon, Lord, 49
electorate, 23, 28, 146, 173 n. 58, 184 n. 16
Ellesmere, Lord, 155

emperor, 59, 80, 81, 102, 122, 125, 130, 155, 175 n. 8; condemnation of, 56; deposition of, 56; not bound by the laws, 56
empire, 82, 122; Carolingian, 133; Frankish, 82; German, 50; neo-Roman, 80, 91; Roman, 12, 32, 41, 43, 56, 73, 74, 80, 82, 90, 110, 121, 122, 125, 142, 177 n. 14; Roman-German, 50, 80, 91, 100, 102; universal, 90, 91
enactment, 14, 149; inhuman, 30
Enclosure act, 24
England, 1–4, 6–8, 11, 14–18, 22, 25, 26, 28, 31–41, 43–45, 47, 49–51, 53, 58, 60, 62, 64, 65, 69, 71–73, 75–77, 79, 82, 84, 86, 88, 93–95, 97–101, 104, 105, 114–116, 120–126, 131, 134, 136, 137, 141, 142, 145, 147, 149–151, 153–157, 159, 160, 162–165, 167, 168, 169 n. 4, 170 n. 15, 173 n. 60, 174 n. 64, 177 n. 18, 182 n. 2, 183 n. 11, 185 n. 18, 188 n. 46 and n. 48.
enlightenment, 42, 43, 49, 83, 90, 102, 152, 157, 165
enrolment, 95
epuration, political, 140
equality, economic, 152; formal, 176 n. 11; legal, 43, 92, 143, 152
equity, 45, 49, 69, 87, 120, 128; married woman's, 87; uncodified, 43
establishment, judicial 134, 154; legal, 7, 47, 100; political, 53, 158
estates, 102, 113; General, 103; provincial, 103
Etats généraux, 105, 107
Europe, Continent, 1, 2, 10, 12, 16–18, 20, 26, 31–39, 41, 44, 47, 48, 50, 53, 54, 57, 58, 64, 65, 67, 71–73, 75, 81–84, 90, 91, 93, 95, 97, 108, 109, 111, 113, 114, 117, 119, 121–126, 133–135, 137, 138, 144, 145, 147, 149, 150, 159, 168, 173 n. 55 and n. 60, 175 n. 8, 177 n. 14, 181 n. 9 and n. 10, 183 n. 11; western, 67, 86, 126, 160, 165, 167

mind, judicial, 17
ministère public, 35
misdemeanour, 133
mistake, 5
moderni, 90
modernisation, 7, 84, 88, 98, 114,
117, 118, 126, 157, 165
monarchie féodale, 75
monarchy, 2, 34, 37, 70, 75, 76,
82–85, 94, 100, 108, 113, 116,
143, 146, 147, 149, 150, 152, 155,
157, 176 n. 9, 176 n. 11;
enlightened, 91; Frankish, 36;
French, 104, 105, 107, 115;
restoration of, 7, 9, 46, 79, 154,
188 n. 46; Stuart, 122
monocracy, 82, 83
Montpellier, 70, 155, 185 n. 19
morality, 21
municipium, 91

Naples, 58, 100, 155
Napoleon, emperor, 11, 12, 32, 37,
40, 50, 89, 91, 140, 156
Napoleon III, emperor 92, 141
nation, European, 71; state, 91, 93,
104, 110
National Assembly, 37, 140
'National law service', 162
Netherlands, 37, 38; Austrian, 137;
Republic of the United, 70, 71,
103
Nicholas I, Tsar, 42
nobility, 48, 141, 143, 147, 149, 183
n. 11, 184 n. 11, 184 n. 15
noblesse de robe, 152
nomos, 153
Normandy, 36, 37, 93, 95, 97, 115,
116, 163, 188 n. 45
Novellae, 54
Noy, W., 155

obligation, 60
obscurity of the law, 124
O'Connor, P. M., 188 n. 56
offence, capital, 32, 33; indictable,
35; non-clergyable, 33
office, temporary, 140
Office of Tithes, 78

official, bishop's, 58, 109, 117, 135,
142; elected, 147, 148; of the state,
35
oligarchy, 46, 75, 77, 78, 80, 82, 146,
151, 154, 157, 176 n. 11
Oliver, P. R., 188 n. 57
one-party system, 164
opinion, dissenting, 54, 130; learned,
88, 130; legal, 125; sudden, 187
n. 43
oppression, 73, 164, 167
oracles of the law, 52, 54, 60, 99
ordeal, 36, 115, 136, 144
ordinance, 33, 70, 105
ordo judiciarius, 121, 135
Ordonnance Criminelle, 32
organisation, 109, 165; fiscal, 110;
judicial, 9, 50, 56, 138, 167
Orleans, 106
Otis, James, 29
Ottonian, dynasty, 80
Oxford, 3, 17, 22, 48, 61–63, 68, 73,
166

pagus, 133
Pandectist, 12, 52, 72, 123
Pandects, 12
papacy, 109–111, 122, 130, 157
papyrus rolls, 55
pardon, royal, 150
Paris, 6, 11, 46, 47, 59, 60, 70, 104,
105, 107, 134–136, 139, 143, 149
Parker, Lord, 159
Parlement 11, 105–107, 134, 136,
139, 153, 184 n. 15; of Malines,
136; of Paris, 6, 11, 47, 59, 70,
105, 107, 134–136, 139, 143;
jurisdiction of, 104
Parliament, 2, 22, 45, 75, 76, 84, 85,
95, 100, 103, 104, 122, 138, 146,
150, 155, 157, 164, 168, 173
n. 58; intention of, 18–20; judicial
role of, 9; limits to its power, 26;
omnicompetence of, 21;
omnipotence of, 21, 24;
sovereignty of, 21–25, 28;
supremacy of, 172 n. 40
parliamentarian, 83
parliamentarism, 2

Index

partiality, 158
party, 6, 15, 86, 87; communist, 146; functionary, 87
paterfamilias, 46
patriciate, 77, 148, 160
peace, bourgeois, 92
peasant, 142
Peasants' War, 137
peer, 34
peerage, 149
peers of France, 143
pensionary, 102, 137
performance, specific, 120
Petit-Dutaillis, C., 75
Philip of Alsace, count of Flanders, 148
Philip II Augustus, king of France, 70
Philip IV the Fair, king of France, 110, 143
philosopher-king, 110
philosophy, 63, 72, 145; Greek, 82
physics, laws of, 99
Placentinus, 155
Plantagenet, dynasty, 94, 95, 115
plebs, 160, 176 n.11
plena probatio, 144
Plucknett, T. F. T., 7
podestà, 147, 148
Poitiers, 120
police custody, 38, 39
polis, 91
politics, 19, 28, 68, 90, 93, 98, 106, 108, 109, 146, 150, 158, 163, 176 n.13, 177 n.18, 180 n.8
Pollock, F., 17, 29
Polnoe Sobranie Zakonov 42
polyandry, 31
polygamy, 31
Portalis, J. E. M., 51
Pothier, Robert-Joseph, 70, 107, 108
Pound, Roscoe, 68, 96, 153
power, absolute, 22; arbitrary, 25, 98; discretionary, 47; executive, 139; imperial, 155; judicial, 150; political, 146, 155, 179 n.41; -struggle, 108
praetor, 125
precedent, 10, 14, 21, 60, 61, 69, 71, 77, 86, 87, 95, 97, 98, 161, 174

n.62, 180 n.42, 187 n.43; awkward, 96; bad, 49, 50, 128, 129, 174 n.68, 178 n.29, 182 n.2; new, 154; old, 154, 174 n.68; reasonable, 182 n.3; reversed, 129
préliminaire de conciliation, 156
prematureness, 7, 46, 47
President of the United States, 151
pressure group, 68
presumption, legal, 173 n.61
preuves légales, 37, 144
preuves savantes, 37, 144
Prime Minister, 150, 186 n.30
prince not bound by laws, 73
principality, 11, 84, 100–102, 104
principles, general, 152
private members' bills, 24
privilege, 33, 152–154; ecclesiastical, 116
privilege *de non appellando*, 102; *de non evocando*, 102
privilegium fori, 32
procedure, 37, 58, 94, 114, 117, 121, 126, 133, 135, 153; civil, 50; code of, 43; cost of, 137; criminal, 32, 34, 38, 48, 165, code of, 32; democratic, 177 n.16; *in camera*, 133, 159; in open court, 77, 165; learned, 136, 144; professional, 120; rational, 136; Roman-canonical, 5, 36, 37, 58, 59, 107, 116, 120, 135; science of, 135
process, due, 143
procurator fiscal, 34
procurator, of the king, 34, 35
procureur, 35
profession, legal, 7, 62–64, 97, 124, 137, 150, 151, 166; liberal; 166
professionalism, 131–138, 160
professor of law, 12, 13, 52–54, 60, 64, 65, 67, 69, 71, 83–88, 90, 93, 96, 100–102, 106, 108, 111, 125, 155
progress, 49, 154
proletariat, industrial, 92
proof, 36, 115, 116, 144; full 144
property, 26, 48, 74, 79, 92, 139, 147, 153, 154, 176 n.13; married women's, 43; owner, 23